Mastering JavaScript

Explore and master modern JavaScript techniques
in order to build large-scale web applications

Ved Antani

PUBLISHING

BIRMINGHAM - MUMBAI

Mastering JavaScript

First published: January 2016

Production reference: 1250116

Published by Packt Publishing Ltd.
Livery Place
35 Livery Street
Birmingham B3 2PB, UK.

ISBN 978-1-78528-134-1

www.packtpub.com

Credits

Author
Ved Antani

Reviewer
Ivano Malavolta

Commissioning Editor
Sarah Crofton

Acquisition Editor
Kevin Colaco

Content Development Editor
Merint Mathew

Technical Editor
Manthan Raja

Copy Editor
Tasneem Fatehi

Project Coordinator
Francina Pinto

Proofreader
Safis Editing

Indexer
Monica Ajmera Mehta

Production Coordinator
Conidon Miranda

Cover Work
Conidon Miranda

About the Author

Ved Antani is an AVP (engineering) at Myntra. Before Myntra, he worked with Electronic Arts, NetApp, and Oracle. Ved is passionate about programming and has been programming in JavaScript since 2005. He has extensive experience in building scalable systems and mobile applications. Ved is a minimalist, a father, and an avid tea drinker.

I would like to thank my wife, Meghna, for her support. She was always there to encourage and help me when I needed it the most.

About the Reviewer

Ivano Malavolta is a postdoctoral researcher at the Gran Sasso Science Institute (L'Aquila, Italy), and he holds a PhD in computer science from the University of L'Aquila. His research is positioned in three main fields: software architecture, Model-Driven Engineering (MDE), and mobile-enabled systems. He is especially interested in investigating how MDE techniques can be exploited for architecting complex and mobile-enabled software systems at the right level of abstraction. He is the author of more than 40 papers in international journals and peer-reviewed international conferences' proceedings; among them, he has coauthored two articles published in the IEEE Transactions on Software Engineering (TSE), which is considered the leading journal in the field of software engineering. He is a reviewer for four international journals, a program committee member of 10 international conferences, a reviewer for 13 international conferences, and a guest editor of an international journal.

He is an instructor of three courses on software engineering, mobile computing, and mobile application development via web technologies; these courses are held at the University of L'Aquila and Gran Sasso Science Institute, Italy.

He has previously reviewed other books about web technologies for Packt Publishing, such as *Backbone.js Cookbook* by *Vadim Mirgorod* and *Backbone.js Blueprints* by *Andrew Burgess*.

www.PacktPub.com

Support files, eBooks, discount offers, and more

For support files and downloads related to your book, please visit www.PacktPub.com.

Did you know that Packt offers eBook versions of every book published, with PDF and ePub files available? You can upgrade to the eBook version at www.PacktPub.com and as a print book customer, you are entitled to a discount on the eBook copy. Get in touch with us at service@packtpub.com for more details.

At www.PacktPub.com, you can also read a collection of free technical articles, sign up for a range of free newsletters and receive exclusive discounts and offers on Packt books and eBooks.

https://www2.packtpub.com/books/subscription/packtlib

Do you need instant solutions to your IT questions? PacktLib is Packt's online digital book library. Here, you can search, access, and read Packt's entire library of books.

Why subscribe?

- Fully searchable across every book published by Packt
- Copy and paste, print, and bookmark content
- On demand and accessible via a web browser

Free access for Packt account holders

If you have an account with Packt at www.PacktPub.com, you can use this to access PacktLib today and view 9 entirely free books. Simply use your login credentials for immediate access.

Table of Contents

Preface   vii

Chapter 1: JavaScript Primer   1

A little bit of history   2
How to use this book   3
Hello World   6
An overview of JavaScript   6
Comments   6
Variables   7
Constants   7
Number   8
String   11
Undefined values   13
Booleans   13
The instanceof operator   15
Date objects   15
The + operator   16
The ++ and -- operators   17
Boolean operators   18
Equality   25
JavaScript types   27
Automatic semicolon insertion   30
JavaScript style guide   32
Whitespaces   32
Parentheses, line breaks, and braces   32
Quotes   34
End of lines and empty lines   34
Type checking   35
Type casting   35
Conditional evaluation   36
Naming   38

The eval() method is evil	39
The strict mode	39
Running JSHint	41
Summary	**43**
Chapter 2: Functions, Closures, and Modules	**45**
A function literal	**46**
A function declaration	46
Functions as data	**49**
Scoping	**50**
Global scope	51
Local scope	52
Function-level scope versus block-level scope	52
Inline function expressions	56
Block scopes	56
Function declarations versus function expressions	**58**
The arguments parameter	**60**
The this parameter	61
Invocation as a function	61
Invocation as a method	61
Invocation as a constructor	63
Invocation using apply() and call() methods	63
Anonymous functions	**64**
Anonymous functions while creating an object	64
Anonymous functions while creating a list	64
Anonymous functions as a parameter to another function	65
Anonymous functions in conditional logic	65
Closures	**66**
Timers and callbacks	**69**
Private variables	**69**
Loops and closures	**70**
Modules	**71**
Stylistic considerations	72
Summary	**73**
Chapter 3: Data Structures and Manipulation	**75**
Regular expressions	**76**
Exact match	**77**
Match from a class of characters	**77**
Repeated occurrences	**81**
Alternatives – OR	84
Beginning and end	**84**

Backreferences	**84**
Greedy and lazy quantifiers	**85**
Arrays	**86**
Maps	**95**
Sets	**95**
A matter of style	**97**
Summary	**97**
Chapter 4: Object-Oriented JavaScript	**99**
Understanding objects	**99**
Behavior of JavaScript objects	101
Prototypes	103
Instance properties versus prototype properties	**104**
Inheritance	**110**
Getters and setters	**117**
Summary	**120**
Chapter 5: JavaScript Patterns	**121**
Design patterns	**122**
The namespace pattern	**123**
The module pattern	**124**
ES6 modules	131
The factory pattern	**131**
The mixin pattern	**133**
The decorator pattern	**134**
The observer pattern	**137**
JavaScript Model-View-* patterns	**139**
Model-View-Controller	139
Models	140
Views	140
Controllers	141
The Model-View-Presenter pattern	**141**
Model-View-ViewModel	**142**
Summary	**143**
Chapter 6: Testing and Debugging	**145**
Unit testing	**146**
Test-driven development	147
Behavior-driven development	147
JavaScript debugging	**154**
Syntax errors	154
Using strict	155

Runtime exceptions	155
Console.log and asserts	156
Chrome DevTools	157
Summary	**162**
Chapter 7: ECMAScript 6	**163**
Shims or polyfills	**164**
Transpilers	**164**
ES6 syntax changes	**165**
Block scoping	165
Default parameters	167
Spread and rest	167
Destructuring	168
Object literals	170
Template literals	171
Maps and Sets	172
Symbols	175
Iterators	175
For..of loops	176
Arrow functions	176
Summary	**179**
Chapter 8: DOM Manipulation and Events	**181**
DOM	**181**
Accessing DOM elements	182
Accessing specific nodes	183
Chaining	**191**
Traversal and manipulation	**191**
Working with browser events	**193**
Propagation	**194**
jQuery event handling and propagation	**195**
Event delegation	**198**
The event object	**199**
Summary	**200**
Chapter 9: Server-Side JavaScript	**201**
An asynchronous evented-model in a browser	**202**
Callbacks	**206**
Timers	**210**
EventEmitters	**211**
Modules	**212**
Creating modules	213

npm   215
  Installing packages   216
JavaScript performance   218
  JavaScript profiling   218
    The CPU profile   219
    The Timeline view   220
Summary   222
Index   223

Preface

It would seem that everything that needs to be written about JavaScript has been written. Frankly, it is difficult to find a topic related to JavaScript that has not been discussed ad nauseam. However, JavaScript is changing at a rapid pace. ECMAScript 6 has the potential to transform the language and how we code in it. Node.js has already changed the way in which we write servers in JavaScript. Newer ideas such as React and Flux will drive the next iteration of the language. While we spend our time learning the new features, there is no denying that the foundational ideas of JavaScript have to be mastered. These ideas are fundamental and need attention. If you are already an experienced JavaScript developer, you will realize that modern JavaScript is vastly different from the language that most people have known. Modern JavaScript demands a specific stylistic discipline and rigor of thought. Tools are more powerful and slowly becoming an integral part of the development workflow. Though the language seems to be changing, it is built on some very solid and constant ideas. This book emphasizes on these fundamental ideas.

While the book was being written, things kept changing in the JavaScript landscape. Luckily, we were able to include all the important and relevant updates in this book.

Mastering JavaScript provides you with a detailed overview of the language's fundamentals and some of the modern tools and libraries, such as jQuery, Underscore.js, and Jasmine.

We hope that you enjoy this book as much as we enjoyed writing it.

What this book covers

Chapter 1, JavaScript Primer, focuses on the language constructs without spending too much time on the basic details. We will cover the trickier parts of variable scoping and loops and best practices for using types and data structures. We will also cover a lot of ground on the coding style and recommended code organization patterns.

Chapter 2, Functions, Closures and Modules, covers the core of the language intricacies. We will discuss the complexities involved in using functional aspects with different treatment for closures in JavaScript. This is a careful and elaborate discussion that will prepare you to explore more advanced design patterns further on.

Chapter 3, Data Structures and Manipulation, takes a detailed look at regular expressions and arrays. Arrays are a fundamental data type in JavaScript and this chapter will help you work effectively with arrays. Regular expressions can make your code concise — we will take a detailed look at how to use RegEx effectively in your code.

Chapter 4, Object-Oriented JavaScript, discusses object orientation in JavaScript. We will discuss inheritance and the prototype chain and focus on understanding the prototypal inheritance model that JavaScript offers. We will also discuss how different this model is from other object-oriented models to help Java or C++ programmers get familiarized with the change.

Chapter 5, JavaScript Patterns, discusses common design patterns and how to implement them in JavaScript. Once you master the object-oriented model for JavaScript, it is easier to understand design and programming patterns to write modular and easy-to-maintain code.

Chapter 6, Testing and Debugging, covers various modern methods to test and debug issues in JavaScript code. We will also explore continuous testing and test-driven methodologies for JavaScript. We will use Jasmine as the test framework.

Chapter 7, ECMAScript 6, focuses on the newer language features introduced by ECMAScript 6 (ES6). It makes JavaScript more powerful and this chapter will help you understand the newer features and how to use them in your code.

Chapter 8, DOM Manipulation and Events, takes a detailed look at JavaScript as a language of the browser. This chapter discusses DOM manipulation and browser events.

Chapter 9, Server-Side JavaScript, explains how we can use Node.js to write scalable server systems in JavaScript. We will discuss the architecture of Node.js and several useful techniques.

What you need for this book

All the examples in this book can be run on any modern browser. For the last chapter, you will need Node.js. You will need the following prerequisites to run the examples and samples from this book:

- A computer with Windows 7 or higher, Linux, or Mac OS X installed.

- The latest version of the Google Chrome or Mozilla Firefox browser.

- A text editor of your choice. Sublime Text, vi, Atom, or Notepad++ would be ideal. The choice is entirely yours.

Who this book is for

This book is intended to equip you with the details necessary to master JavaScript. This book will be useful for the following audience:

- Experienced developers familiar with other object-oriented languages. Information in this book will enable them to transition to JavaScript using their existing experience.

- Web developers with some amount of experience with JavaScript. This book will help them learn advanced concepts of JavaScript and refine their programming style.

- Beginners who want to understand and eventually master JavaScript. This book has the necessary information for them to get started.

Conventions

In this book, you will find a number of text styles that distinguish between different kinds of information. Here are some examples of these styles and an explanation of their meaning.

Code words in text, database table names, folder names, filenames, file extensions, pathnames, dummy URLs, user input, and Twitter handles are shown as follows: "First, the `<script>` tag in `<head>` imports JavaScript, while the second `<script>` tag is used to embed inline JavaScript."

A block of code is set as follows:

```
function sayHello(what) {
  return "Hello " + what;
}
console.log(sayHello("world"));
```

When we wish to draw your attention to a particular part of a code block, the relevant lines or items are set in bold:

```
<head>
  <script type="text/javascript" src="script.js"></script>
  <script type="text/javascript">
    var x = "Hello World";
    console.log(x);
  </script>
</head>
```

Any command-line input or output is written as follows:

```
EN-VedA:~$ node
> 0.1+0.2
0.30000000000000004
> (0.1+0.2)===0.3
false
```

New terms and **important words** are shown in bold. Words that you see on the screen, for example, in menus or dialog boxes, appear in the text like this: "You can run the page and inspect using Chrome's **Developer Tool**"

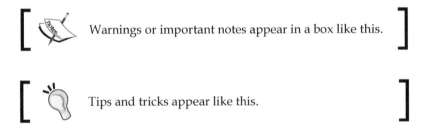

Warnings or important notes appear in a box like this.

Tips and tricks appear like this.

Reader feedback

Feedback from our readers is always welcome. Let us know what you think about this book—what you liked or disliked. Reader feedback is important for us as it helps us develop titles that you will really get the most out of.

To send us general feedback, simply e-mail feedback@packtpub.com, and mention the book's title in the subject of your message.

If there is a topic that you have expertise in and you are interested in either writing or contributing to a book, see our author guide at www.packtpub.com/authors.

Customer support

Now that you are the proud owner of a Packt book, we have a number of things to help you to get the most from your purchase.

Downloading the example code

You can download the example code files from your account at `http://www.packtpub.com` for all the Packt Publishing books you have purchased. If you purchased this book elsewhere, you can visit `http://www.packtpub.com/support` and register to have the files e-mailed directly to you.

Downloading the color images of this book

We also provide you with a PDF file that has color images of the screenshots/ diagrams used in this book. The color images will help you better understand the changes in the output. You can download this file from `https://www.packtpub.com/sites/default/files/downloads/MasteringJavaScript_ColorImages.pdf`.

Errata

Although we have taken every care to ensure the accuracy of our content, mistakes do happen. If you find a mistake in one of our books—maybe a mistake in the text or the code—we would be grateful if you could report this to us. By doing so, you can save other readers from frustration and help us improve subsequent versions of this book. If you find any errata, please report them by visiting `http://www.packtpub.com/submit-errata`, selecting your book, clicking on the **Errata Submission Form** link, and entering the details of your errata. Once your errata are verified, your submission will be accepted and the errata will be uploaded to our website or added to any list of existing errata under the Errata section of that title.

To view the previously submitted errata, go to `https://www.packtpub.com/books/content/support` and enter the name of the book in the search field. The required information will appear under the **Errata** section.

Piracy

Piracy of copyrighted material on the Internet is an ongoing problem across all media. At Packt, we take the protection of our copyright and licenses very seriously. If you come across any illegal copies of our works in any form on the Internet, please provide us with the location address or website name immediately so that we can pursue a remedy.

Please contact us at `copyright@packtpub.com` with a link to the suspected pirated material.

We appreciate your help in protecting our authors and our ability to bring you valuable content.

Questions

If you have a problem with any aspect of this book, you can contact us at `questions@packtpub.com`, and we will do our best to address the problem.

1
JavaScript Primer

It is always difficult to pen the first few words, especially on a subject like JavaScript. This difficulty arises primarily because so many things have been said about this language. JavaScript has been the *Language of the Web*—lingua franca, if you will, since the earliest days of the Netscape Navigator. JavaScript went from a tool of the amateur to the weapon of the connoisseur in a shockingly short period of time.

JavaScript is the most popular language on the web and open source ecosystem. `http://githut.info/` charts the number of active repositories and overall popularity of the language on GitHub for the last few years. JavaScript's popularity and importance can be attributed to its association with the browser. Google's V8 and Mozilla's SpiderMonkey are extremely optimized JavaScript engines that power Google Chrome and Mozilla Firefox browsers, respectively.

Although web browsers are the most widely used platforms for JavaScript, modern databases such as MongoDB and CouchDB use JavaScript as their scripting and query language. JavaScript has become an important platform outside browsers as well. Projects such as **Node.js** and **io.js** provide powerful platforms to develop scalable server environments using JavaScript. Several interesting projects are pushing the language capabilities to its limits, for example, **Emscripten** (`http://kripken.github.io/emscripten-site/`) is a **Low-Level Virtual Machine (LLVM)**-based project that compiles C and C++ into highly optimizable JavaScript in an **asm. js** format. This allows you to run C and C++ on the web at near native speed.

JavaScript is built around solid foundations regarding, for example, functions, dynamic objects, loose typing, prototypal inheritance, and a powerful object literal notation.

While JavaScript is built on sound design principles, unfortunately, the language had to evolve along with the browser. Web browsers are notorious in the way they support various features and standards. JavaScript tried to accommodate all the whims of the browsers and ended up making some very bad design decisions. These bad parts (the term made famous by Douglas Crockford) overshadowed the good parts of the language for most people. Programmers wrote bad code, other programmers had nightmares trying to debug that bad code, and the language eventually got a bad reputation. Unfortunately, JavaScript is one of the most misunderstood programming languages (`http://javascript.crockford.com/javascript.html`).

Another criticism leveled at JavaScript is that it lets you get things done without you being an expert in the language. I have seen programmers write exceptionally bad JavaScript code just because they wanted to get the things done quickly and JavaScript allowed them to do just this. I have spent hours debugging very bad quality JavaScript written by someone who clearly was not a programmer. However, the language is a tool and cannot be blamed for sloppy programming. Like all crafts, programming demands extreme dedication and discipline.

A little bit of history

In 1993, the **Mosaic** browser of **National Center for Supercomputing Applications** (**NCSA**) was one of the first popular web browsers. A year later, Netscape Communications created the proprietary web browser, **Netscape Navigator**. Several original Mosaic authors worked on Navigator.

In 1995, Netscape Communications hired Brendan Eich with the promise of letting him implement **Scheme** (a Lisp dialect) in the browser. Before this happened, Netscape got in touch with Sun Microsystems (now Oracle) to include Java in the Navigator browser.

Due to the popularity and easy programming of Java, Netscape decided that a scripting language had to have a syntax similar to that of Java. This ruled out adopting existing languages such as Python, **Tool Command Language** (**TCL**), or Scheme. Eich wrote the initial prototype in just 10 days (`http://www.computer.org/csdl/mags/co/2012/02/mco2012020007.pdf`), in May 1995. JavaScript's first code name was **Mocha**, coined by Marc Andreessen. Netscape later changed it to **LiveScript**, for trademark reasons. In early December 1995, Sun licensed the trademark Java to Netscape. The language was renamed to its final name, JavaScript.

How to use this book

This book is not going to help if you are looking to get things done quickly. This book is going to focus on the correct ways to code in JavaScript. We are going to spend a lot of time understanding how to avoid the bad parts of the language and build reliable and readable code in JavaScript. We will skirt away from sloppy features of the language just to make sure that you are not getting used to them — if you have already learned to code using these habits, this book will try to nudge you away from this. There will be a lot of focus on the correct style and tools to make your code better.

Most of the concepts in this book are going to be examples and patterns from real-world problems. I will insist that you code each of the snippets to make sure that your understanding of the concept is getting programmed into your muscle memory. Trust me on this, there is no better way to learn programming than writing a lot of code.

Typically, you will need to create an HTML page to run an embedded JavaScript code as follows:

```html
<!DOCTYPE html>
<html>
<head>
  <script type="text/javascript" src="script.js"></script>
  <script type="text/javascript">
    var x = "Hello World";
    console.log(x);
  </script>
</head>
<body>
</body>
</html>
```

This sample code shows two ways in which JavaScript is embedded into the HTML page. First, the `<script>` tag in `<head>` imports JavaScript, while the second `<script>` tag is used to embed inline JavaScript.

> **Downloading the example code**
>
> You can download the example code files from your account at `http://www.packtpub.com` for all the Packt Publishing books you have purchased. If you purchased this book elsewhere, you can visit `http://www.packtpub.com/support` and register to have the files e-mailed directly to you.

You can save this HTML page locally and open it in a browser. On Firefox, you can open the **Developer** console (Firefox menu | **Developer** | **Web Console**) and you can see the **"Hello World"** text on the **Console** tab. Based on your OS and browser version, the screen may look different:

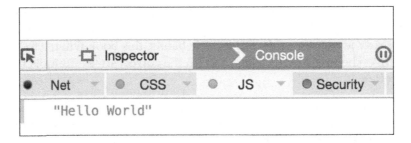

You can run the page and inspect it using Chrome's **Developer Tool**:

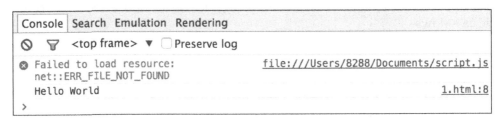

A very interesting thing to notice here is that there is an error displayed on the console regarding the missing .js file that we are trying to import using the following line of code:

```
<script type="text/javascript" src="script.js"></script>
```

Using browser developer consoles or an extension such as **Firebug** can be very useful in debugging error conditions in the code. We will discuss in detail the debugging techniques in later chapters.

Creating such HTML scaffolds can be tedious for every exercise in this book. Instead, we want to use a **Read-Eval-Print-Loop (REPL)** for JavaScript. Unlike Python, JavaScript does not come packaged with an REPL. We can use Node.js as an REPL. If you have Node.js installed on your machine, you can just type node on the command line and start experimenting with it. You will observe that Node REPL errors are not very elegantly displayed.

Let's see the following example:

```
EN-VedA:~$ node
>function greeter(){
  x="World"1
SyntaxError: Unexpected identifier
    at Object.exports.createScript (vm.js:44:10)
    at REPLServer.defaultEval (repl.js:117:23)
    at bound (domain.js:254:14)

    ...
```

After this error, you will have to restart. Still, it can help you try out small fragments of code a lot faster.

Another tool that I personally use a lot is **JS Bin** (`http://jsbin.com/`). JS Bin provides you with a great set of tools to test JavaScript, such as syntax highlighting and runtime error detection. The following is a screenshot of JS Bin:

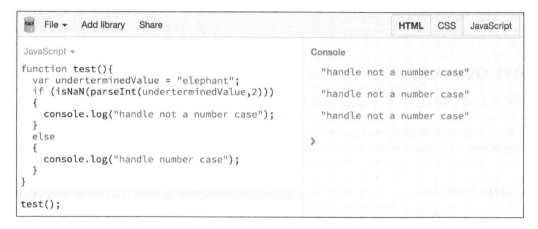

Based on your preference, you can pick the tool that makes it easier to try out the code samples. Regardless of which tool you use, make sure that you type out every exercise in this book.

Hello World

No programming language should be published without a customary Hello World program — why should this book be any different?

Type (don't copy and paste) the following code in JS Bin:

```
function sayHello(what) {
  return "Hello " + what;
}
console.log(sayHello("world"));
```

Your screen should look something as follows:

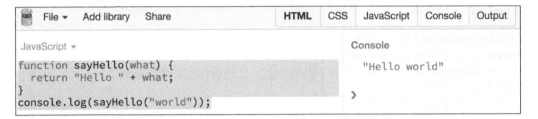

An overview of JavaScript

In a nutshell, JavaScript is a prototype-based scripting language with dynamic typing and first-class function support. JavaScript borrows most of its syntax from Java, but is also influenced by Awk, Perl, and Python. JavaScript is case-sensitive and white space-agnostic.

Comments

JavaScript allows single line or multiple line comments. The syntax is similar to C or Java:

```
// a one line comment

/* this is a longer,
   multi-line comment
 */

/* You can't /* nest comments */ SyntaxError */
```

Variables

Variables are symbolic names for values. The names of variables, or identifiers, must follow certain rules.

A JavaScript variable name must start with a letter, underscore (_), or dollar sign ($); subsequent characters can also be digits (0-9). As JavaScript is case sensitive, letters include the characters *A* through *Z* (uppercase) and the characters *a* through *z* (lowercase).

You can use ISO 8859-1 or Unicode letters in variable names.

New variables in JavaScript should be defined with the **var** keyword. If you declare a variable without assigning a value to it, its type is undefined by default. One terrible thing is that if you don't declare your variable with the var keyword, they become implicit globals. Let me reiterate that implicit globals are a terrible thing — we will discuss this in detail later in the book when we discuss variable scopes and closures, but it's important to remember that you should always declare a variable with the var keyword unless you know what you are doing:

```
var a;        //declares a variable but its undefined
var b = 0;
console.log(b);     //0
console.log(a);     //undefined
console.log(a+b);   //NaN
```

The NaN value is a special value that indicates that the entity is *not a number*.

Constants

You can create a read-only named constant with the **const** keyword. The constant name must start with a letter, underscore, or dollar sign and can contain alphabetic, numeric, or underscore characters:

```
const area_code = '515';
```

A constant cannot change the value through assignment or be redeclared, and it has to be initialized to a value.

JavaScript supports the standard variations of types:

- Number
- String
- Boolean
- Symbol (new in ECMAScript 6)
- Object:
    - ○ Function
    - ○ Array
    - ○ Date
    - ○ RegExp
- Null
- Undefined

Number

The **Number** type can represent both 32-bit integer and 64-bit floating point values. For example, the following line of code declares a variable to hold an integer value, which is defined by the literal 555:

```
var aNumber = 555;
```

To define a floating point value, you need to include a decimal point and one digit after the decimal point:

```
var aFloat = 555.0;
```

Essentially, there's no such thing as an integer in JavaScript. JavaScript uses a 64-bit floating point representation, which is the same as Java's double.

Hence, you would see something as follows:

```
EN-VedA:~$ node
> 0.1+0.2
0.30000000000000004
> (0.1+0.2)===0.3
false
```

I recommend that you read the exhaustive answer on Stack Overflow (http://stackoverflow.com/questions/588004/is-floating-point-math-broken) and (http://floating-point-gui.de/), which explains why this is the case. However, it is important to understand that floating point arithmetic should be handled with due care. In most cases, you will not have to rely on extreme precision of decimal points but if you have to, you can try using libraries such as **big.js** (https://github.com/MikeMcl/big.js) that try to solve this problem.

If you intend to code extremely precise financial systems, you should represent $ values as cents to avoid rounding errors. One of the systems that I worked on used to round off the **Value Added Tax (VAT)** amount to two decimal points. With thousands of orders a day, this rounding off amount per order became a massive accounting headache. We needed to overhaul the entire Java web service stack and JavaScript frontend for this.

A few special values are also defined as part of the Number type. The first two are `Number.MAX_VALUE` and `Number.MIN_VALUE`, which define the outer bounds of the Number value set. All ECMAScript numbers must fall between these two values, without exception. A calculation can, however, result in a number that does not fall in between these two numbers. When a calculation results in a number greater than `Number.MAX_VALUE`, it is assigned a value of `Number.POSITIVE_INFINITY`, meaning that it has no numeric value anymore. Likewise, a calculation that results in a number less than `Number.MIN_VALUE` is assigned a value of `Number.NEGATIVE_INFINITY`, which also has no numeric value. If a calculation returns an infinite value, the result cannot be used in any further calculations. You can use the `isInfinite()` method to verify if the calculation result is an infinity.

Another peculiarity of JavaScript is a special value called NaN (short for *Not a Number*). In general, this occurs when conversion from another type (String, Boolean, and so on) fails. Observe the following peculiarity of NaN:

```
EN-VedA:~ $ node
> isNaN(NaN);
true
> NaN==NaN;
false
> isNaN("elephant");
true
> NaN+5;
NaN
```

The second line is strange—NaN is not equal to NaN. If NaN is part of any mathematical operation, the result also becomes NaN. As a general rule, stay away from using NaN in any expression. For any advanced mathematical operations, you can use the `Math` global object and its methods:

```
> Math.E
2.718281828459045
> Math.SQRT2
1.4142135623730951
> Math.abs(-900)
900
> Math.pow(2,3)
8
```

You can use the `parseInt()` and `parseFloat()` methods to convert a string expression to an integer or float:

```
> parseInt("230",10);
230
> parseInt("010",10);
10
> parseInt("010",8); //octal base
8
> parseInt("010",2); //binary
2
> + "4"
4
```

With `parseInt()`, you should provide an explicit base to prevent nasty surprises on older browsers. The last trick is just using a + sign to auto-convert the `"42"` string to a number, `42`. It is also prudent to handle the `parseInt()` result with `isNaN()`. Let's see the following example:

```
var underterminedValue = "elephant";
if (isNaN(parseInt(underterminedValue,2)))
{
    console.log("handle not a number case");
}
else
{
    console.log("handle number case");
}
```

In this example, you are not sure of the type of the value that the `underterminedValue` variable can hold if the value is being set from an external interface. If `isNaN()` is not handled, `parseInt()` will cause an exception and the program can crash.

String

In JavaScript, strings are a sequence of Unicode characters (each character takes 16 bits). Each character in the string can be accessed by its index. The first character index is zero. Strings are enclosed inside " or ' —both are valid ways to represent strings. Let's see the following:

```
> console.log("Hippopotamus chewing gum");
Hippopotamus chewing gum
> console.log('Single quoted hippopotamus');
Single quoted hippopotamus
> console.log("Broken \n lines");
Broken
 lines
```

The last line shows you how certain character literals when escaped with a backslash \ can be used as special characters. The following is a list of such special characters:

- \n: Newline
- \t: Tab
- \b: Backspace
- \r: Carriage return
- \\: Backslash
- \': Single quote
- \": Double quote

You get default support for special characters and Unicode literals with JavaScript strings:

```
> '\xA9'
'©'
> '\u00A9'
'©'
```

One important thing about JavaScript Strings, Numbers, and Booleans is that they actually have wrapper objects around their primitive equivalent. The following example shows the usage of the wrapper objects:

```
var s = new String("dummy"); //Creates a String object
console.log(s); //"dummy"
console.log(typeof s); //"object"
var nonObject = "1" + "2"; //Create a String primitive
console.log(typeof nonObject); //"string"
var objString = new String("1" + "2"); //Creates a String object
console.log(typeof objString); //"object"
//Helper functions
console.log("Hello".length); //5
console.log("Hello".charAt(0)); //"H"
console.log("Hello".charAt(1)); //"e"
console.log("Hello".indexOf("e")); //1
console.log("Hello".lastIndexOf("l")); //3
console.log("Hello".startsWith("H")); //true
console.log("Hello".endsWith("o")); //true
console.log("Hello".includes("X")); //false
var splitStringByWords = "Hello World".split(" ");
console.log(splitStringByWords); //["Hello", "World"]
var splitStringByChars = "Hello World".split("");
console.log(splitStringByChars); //["H", "e", "l", "l", "o", " ",
   "W", "o", "r", "l", "d"]
console.log("lowercasestring".toUpperCase()); //"LOWERCASESTRING"
console.log("UPPPERCASESTRING".toLowerCase());
   //"upppercasestring"
console.log("There are no spaces in the end    ".trim());
   //"There are no spaces in the end"
```

JavaScript allows multiline strings also. Strings enclosed within ` (Grave accent— https://en.wikipedia.org/wiki/Grave_accent) are considered multiline. Let's see the following example:

```
> console.log(`string text on first line
string text on second line `);
"string text on first line
string text on second line "
```

This kind of string is also known as a template string and can be used for string interpolation. JavaScript allows Python-like string interpolation using this syntax.

Normally, you would do something similar to the following:

```
var a=1, b=2;
console.log("Sum of values is :" + (a+b) + " and multiplication is :"
  + (a*b));
```

However, with string interpolation, things become a bit clearer:

```
console.log(`Sum of values is :${a+b} and multiplication is :
  ${a*b}`);
```

Undefined values

JavaScript indicates an absence of meaningful values by two special values—null, when the non-value is deliberate, and undefined, when the value is not assigned to the variable yet. Let's see the following example:

```
> var xl;
> console.log(typeof xl);
undefined
> console.log(null==undefined);
true
```

Booleans

JavaScript Boolean primitives are represented by `true` and `false` keywords. The following rules govern what becomes false and what turns out to be true:

- False, 0, the empty string (""), NaN, null, and undefined are represented as false
- Everything else is true

JavaScript Booleans are tricky primarily because the behavior is radically different in the way you create them.

There are two ways in which you can create Booleans in JavaScript:

- You can create primitive Booleans by assigning a true or false literal to a variable. Consider the following example:
  ```
  var pBooleanTrue = true;
  var pBooleanFalse = false;
  ```

- Use the `Boolean()` function; this is an ordinary function that returns a primitive Boolean:

```
var fBooleanTrue = Boolean(true);
var fBooleanFalse = Boolean(false);
```

Both these methods return expected *truthy* or *falsy* values. However, if you create a Boolean object using the `new` operator, things can go really wrong.

Essentially, when you use the `new` operator and the `Boolean(value)` constructor, you don't get a primitive `true` or `false` in return, you get an object instead—and unfortunately, JavaScript considers an object as *truthy*:

```
var oBooleanTrue = new Boolean(true);
var oBooleanFalse = new Boolean(false);
console.log(oBooleanTrue); //true
console.log(typeof oBooleanTrue); //object
if(oBooleanFalse){
  console.log("I am seriously truthy, don't believe me");
}
>"I am seriously truthy, don't believe me"


if(oBooleanTrue){
  console.log("I am also truthy, see ?");
}
>"I am also truthy, see ?"


//Use valueOf() to extract real value within the Boolean object
if(oBooleanFalse.valueOf()){
  console.log("With valueOf, I am false");
}else{
  console.log("Without valueOf, I am still truthy");
}
>"Without valueOf, I am still truthy"
```

So, the smart thing to do is to always avoid Boolean constructors to create a new Boolean object. It breaks the fundamental contract of Boolean logic and you should stay away from such difficult-to-debug buggy code.

The instanceof operator

One of the problems with using reference types to store values has been the use of the **typeof** operator, which returns `object` no matter what type of object is being referenced. To provide a solution, you can use the **instanceof** operator. Let's see some examples:

```
var aStringObject = new String("string");
console.log(typeof aStringObject);          //"object"
console.log(aStringObject instanceof String);     //true
var aString = "This is a string";
console.log(aString instanceof String);      //false
```

The third line returns `false`. We will discuss why this is the case when we discuss prototype chains.

Date objects

JavaScript does not have a date data type. Instead, you can use the **Date** object and its methods to work with dates and times in your applications. A Date object is pretty exhaustive and contains several methods to handle most date- and time-related use cases.

JavaScript treats dates similarly to Java. JavaScript store dates as the number of milliseconds since January 1, 1970, 00:00:00.

You can create a Date object using the following declaration:

```
var dataObject = new Date([parameters]);
```

The parameters for the Date object constructors can be as follows:

- No parameters creates today's date and time. For example, `var today = new Date();`.

- A String representing a date as `Month day, year hours:minutes:seconds`. For example, `var twoThousandFifteen = new Date("December 31, 2015 23:59:59");`. If you omit hours, minutes, or seconds, the value will be set to `0`.

- A set of integer values for the year, month, and day. For example, `var christmas = new Date(2015, 11, 25);`.

- A set of integer values for the year, month, day, hour, minute, and seconds. For example, `var christmas = new Date(2015, 11, 25, 21, 00, 0);`.

Here are some examples on how to create and manipulate dates in JavaScript:

```
var today = new Date();
console.log(today.getDate()); //27
console.log(today.getMonth()); //4
console.log(today.getFullYear()); //2015
console.log(today.getHours()); //23
console.log(today.getMinutes()); //13
console.log(today.getSeconds()); //10
//number of milliseconds since January 1, 1970, 00:00:00 UTC
console.log(today.getTime()); //1432748611392
console.log(today.getTimezoneOffset()); //-330 Minutes

//Calculating elapsed time
var start = Date.now();
// loop for a long time
for (var i=0;i<100000;i++);
var end = Date.now();
var elapsed = end - start; // elapsed time in milliseconds
console.log(elapsed); //71
```

For any serious applications that require fine-grained control over date and time objects, we recommend using libraries such as **Moment.js** (`https://github.com/moment/moment`), **Timezone.js** (`https://github.com/mde/timezone-js`), or **date.js** (`https://github.com/MatthewMueller/date`). These libraries simplify a lot of recurrent tasks for you and help you focus on other important things.

The + operator

The + operator, when used as a unary, does not have any effect on a number. However, when applied to a String, the + operator converts it to numbers as follows:

```
var a=25;
a=+a;            //No impact on a's value
console.log(a);  //25

var b="70";
console.log(typeof b); //string
b=+b;            //converts string to number
console.log(b); //70
console.log(typeof b); //number
```

The + operator is used often by a programmer to quickly convert a numeric representation of a String to a number. However, if the String literal is not something that can be converted to a number, you get slightly unpredictable results as follows:

```
var c="foo";
c=+c;                  //Converts foo to number
console.log(c);   //NaN
console.log(typeof c);   //number

var zero="";
zero=+zero; //empty strings are converted to 0
console.log(zero);
console.log(typeof zero);
```

We will discuss the effects of the + operator on several other data types later in the text.

The ++ and -- operators

The ++ operator is a shorthand version of adding 1 to a value and -- is a shorthand to subtract 1 from a value. Java and C have equivalent operators and most will be familiar with them. How about this?

```
var a= 1;
var b= a++;
console.log(a); //2
console.log(b); //1
```

Err, what happened here? Shouldn't the b variable have the value 2? The ++ and -- operators are unary operators that can be used either prefix or postfix. The order in which they are used matters. When ++ is used in the prefix position as ++a, it increments the value before the value is returned from the expression rather than after as with a++. Let's see the following code:

```
var a= 1;
var b= ++a;
console.log(a);   //2
console.log(b);   //2
```

Many programmers use the chained assignments to assign a single value to multiple variables as follows:

```
var a, b, c;
a = b = c = 0;
```

This is fine because the assignment operator (=) results in the value being assigned. In this case, c=0 is evaluated to 0; this would result in b=0, which also evaluates to 0, and hence, a=0 is evaluated.

However, a slight change to the previous example yields extraordinary results. Consider this:

```
var a = b = 0;
```

In this case, only the a variable is declared with var, while the b variable is created as an accidental global. (If you are in the strict mode, you will get an error for this.) With JavaScript, be careful what you wish for, you might get it.

Boolean operators

There are three Boolean operators in JavaScript — AND(&), OR(|), and NOT(!).

Before we discuss logical AND and OR operators, we need to understand how they produce a Boolean result. Logical operators are evaluated from left to right and they are tested using the following short-circuit rules:

- **Logical AND**: If the first operand determines the result, the second operand is not evaluated.

   In the following example, I have highlighted the right-hand side expression if it gets executed as part of short-circuit evaluation rules:

   ```
   console.log(true  && true); // true AND true returns true
   console.log(true  && false);// true AND false returns false
   console.log(false && true);// false AND true returns false
   console.log("Foo" && "Bar");// Foo(true) AND Bar(true)
      returns Bar
   console.log(false && "Foo");// false && Foo(true) returns
      false
   console.log("Foo" && false);// Foo(true) && false returns
      false
   console.log(false && (1 == 2));// false && false(1==2) returns
   false
   ```

- **Logical OR**: If the first operand is true, the second operand is not evaluated:

```
console.log(true  || true); // true AND true returns true
console.log(true  || false);// true AND false returns true
console.log(false || true);// false AND true returns true
console.log("Foo" || "Bar");// Foo(true) AND Bar(true) returns Foo
console.log(false || "Foo");// false && Foo(true) returns Foo
console.log("Foo" || false);// Foo(true) && false returns Foo
console.log(false || (1 == 2));// false && false(1==2) returns
false
```

However, both logical AND and logical OR can also be used for non-Boolean operands. When either the left or right operand is not a primitive Boolean value, AND and OR do not return Boolean values.

Now we will explain the three logical Boolean operators:

- Logical AND(&&): If the first operand object is *falsy*, it returns that object. If its *truthy*, the second operand object is returned:

```
console.log (0 && "Foo");  //First operand is falsy -
   return it
console.log ("Foo" && "Bar"); //First operand is truthy,
   return the second operand
```

- Logical OR(||): If the first operand is *truthy*, it's returned. Otherwise, the second operand is returned:

```
console.log (0 || "Foo");  //First operand is falsy -
   return second operand
console.log ("Foo" || "Bar"); //First operand is truthy,
   return it
console.log (0 || false); //First operand is falsy, return
   second operand
```

The typical use of a logical OR is to assign a default value to a variable:

```
function greeting(name) {
    name = name || "John";
    console.log("Hello " + name);
}

greeting("Johnson"); // alerts "Hi Johnson";
greeting(); //alerts "Hello John"
```

You will see this pattern frequently in most professional JavaScript libraries. You should understand how the defaulting is done by using a logical OR operator.

- **Logical NOT**: This always returns a Boolean value. The value returned depends on the following:

```
//If the operand is an object, false is returned.
var s = new String("string");
console.log(!s);                //false


//If the operand is the number 0, true is returned.
var t = 0;
console.log(!t);                //true


//If the operand is any number other than 0, false is returned.
var x = 11;
console.log(!x);                //false


//If operand is null or NaN, true is returned
var y =null;
var z = NaN;
console.log(!y);                //true
console.log(!z);                //true
//If operand is undefined, you get true
var foo;
console.log(!foo);              //true
```

Additionally, JavaScript supports C-like ternary operators as follows:

```
var allowedToDrive = (age > 21) ? "yes" : "no";
```

If `(age>21)`, the expression after ? will be assigned to the `allowedToDrive` variable and the expression after : is assigned otherwise. This is equivalent to an if-else conditional statement. Let's see another example:

```
function isAllowedToDrive(age){
  if(age>21){
    return true;
  }else{
    return false;
  }
}
console.log(isAllowedToDrive(22));
```

In this example, the `isAllowedToDrive()` function accepts one integer parameter, `age`. Based on the value of this variable, we return true or false to the calling function. This is a well-known and most familiar if-else conditional logic. Most of the time, if-else keeps the code easier to read. For simpler cases of single conditions, using the ternary operator is also okay, but if you see that you are using the ternary operator for more complicated expressions, try to stick with if-else because it is easier to interpret if-else conditions than a very complex ternary expression.

If-else conditional statements can be nested as follows:

```
if (condition1) {
   statement1
} else if (condition2) {
   statement2
} else if (condition3) {
   statement3
}
..
} else {
   statementN
}
```

Purely as a matter of taste, you can indent the nested `else if` as follows:

```
if (condition1) {
   statement1
} else
     if (condition2) {
```

Do not use assignments in place of a conditional statement. Most of the time, they are used because of a mistake as follows:

```
if(a=b) {
   //do something
}
```

Mostly, this happens by mistake; the intended code was `if(a==b)`, or better, `if(a===b)`. When you make this mistake and replace a conditional statement with an assignment statement, you end up committing a very difficult-to-find bug. However, if you really want to use an assignment statement with an if statement, make sure that you make your intentions very clear.

One way is to put extra parentheses around your assignment statement:

```
if((a=b)){
   //this is really something you want to do
}
```

Another way to handle conditional execution is to use switch-case statements. The switch-case construct in JavaScript is similar to that in C or Java. Let's see the following example:

```
function sayDay(day){
   switch(day){
      case 1: console.log("Sunday");
         break;
      case 2: console.log("Monday");
         break;
      default:
         console.log("We live in a binary world. Go to Pluto");
   }
}


sayDay(1); //Sunday
sayDay(3); //We live in a binary world. Go to Pluto
```

One problem with this structure is that you have break out of every case; otherwise, the execution will fall through to the next level. If we remove the break statement from the first case statement, the output will be as follows:

```
>sayDay(1);
Sunday
Monday
```

As you can see, if we omit the break statement to break the execution immediately after a condition is satisfied, the execution sequence follows to the next level. This can lead to difficult-to-detect problems in your code. However, this is also a popular style of writing conditional logic if you intend to fall through to the next level:

```
function debug(level,msg){
   switch(level){
      case "INFO": //intentional fall-through
      case "WARN" :
      case "DEBUG": console.log(level+ ": " + msg);
         break;
      case "ERROR": console.error(msg);
   }
}
```

```
debug("INFO","Info Message");
debug("DEBUG","Debug Message");
debug("ERROR","Fatal Exception");
```

In this example, we are intentionally letting the execution fall through to write a concise switch-case. If levels are either INFO, WARN, or DEBUG, we use the switch-case to fall through to a single point of execution. We omit the `break` statement for this. If you want to follow this pattern of writing switch statements, make sure that you document your usage for better readability.

Switch statements can have a `default` case to handle any value that cannot be evaluated by any other case.

JavaScript has a while and do-while loop. The while loop lets you iterate a set of expressions till a condition is met. The following first example iterates the statements enclosed within {} till the `i<10` expression is true. Remember that if the value of the `i` counter is already greater than `10`, the loop will not execute at all:

```
var i=0;
while(i<10){
    i=i+1;
    console.log(i);
}
```

The following loop keeps executing till infinity because the condition is always true—this can lead to disastrous effects. Your program can use up all your memory or something equally unpleasant:

```
//infinite loop
while(true){
    //keep doing this
}
```

If you want to make sure that you execute the loop at least once, you can use the do-while loop (sometimes known as a post-condition loop):

```
var choice;
do {
    choice=getChoiceFromUserInput();
} while(!isInputValid(input));
```

In this example, we are asking the user for an input till we find a valid input from the user. While the user types invalid input, we keep asking for an input to the user. It is always argued that, logically, every do-while loop can be transformed into a while loop. However, a do-while loop has a very valid use case like the one we just saw where you want the condition to be checked only after there has been one execution of the loop block.

JavaScript has a very powerful loop similar to C or Java—the for loop. The for loop is popular because it allows you to define the control conditions of the loop in a single line.

The following example prints `Hello` five times:

```
for (var i=0;i<5;i++){
  console.log("Hello");
}
```

Within the definition of the loop, you defined the initial value of the loop counter `i` to be `0`, you defined the `i<5` exit condition, and finally, you defined the increment factor.

All three expressions in the previous example are optional. You can omit them if required. For example, the following variations are all going to produce the same result as the previous loop:

```
var x=0;
//Omit initialitzation
for (;x<5;x++){
  console.log("Hello");
}

//Omit exit condition
for (var j=0;;j++){
  //exit condition
  if(j>=5){
    break;
  }else{
    console.log("Hello");
  }
}
//Omit increment
for (var k=0; k<5;){
  console.log("Hello");
  k++;
}
```

You can also omit all three of these expressions and write for loops. One interesting idiom used frequently is to use for loops with empty statements. The following loop is used to set all the elements of the array to `100`. Notice how there is no body to the for-loop:

```
var arr = [10, 20, 30];
// Assign all array values to 100
for (i = 0; i < arr.length; arr[i++] = 100);
console.log(arr);
```

The empty statement here is just the single that we see after the for loop statement. The increment factor also modifies the array content. We will discuss arrays later in the book, but here it's sufficient to see that the array elements are set to the `100` value within the loop definition itself.

Equality

JavaScript offers two modes of equality — strict and loose. Essentially, loose equality will perform the type conversion when comparing two values, while strict equality will check the values without any type conversion. A strict equality check is performed by === while a loose equality check is performed by ==.

ECMAScript 6 also offers the `Object.is` method to do a strict equality check like ===. However, `Object.is` has a special handling for NaN: -0 and +0. When *NaN===NaN* and *NaN==NaN* evaluates to false, `Object.is(NaN,NaN)` will return true.

Strict equality using ===

Strict equality compares two values without any implicit type conversions. The following rules apply:

- If the values are of a different type, they are unequal.
- For non-numerical values of the same type, they are equal if their values are the same.
- For primitive numbers, strict equality works for values. If the values are the same, === results in `true`. However, a NaN doesn't equal to any number and NaN===<a number> would be a `false`.

Strict equality is always the correct equality check to use. Make it a rule to always use === instead of ==:

Condition	Output
`"" === "0"`	false
`0 === ""`	false
`0 === "0"`	false
`false === "false"`	false
`false === "0"`	false
`false === undefined`	false
`false === null`	false
`null === undefined`	false

In case of comparing objects, we get results as follows:

Condition	Output
`{} === {};`	false
`new String('bah') === 'bah';`	false
`new Number(1) === 1;`	false
`var bar = {};` `bar === bar;`	true

The following are further examples that you should try on either JS Bin or Node REPL:

```
var n = 0;
var o = new String("0");
var s = "0";
var b = false;

console.log(n === n); // true - same values for numbers
console.log(o === o); // true - non numbers are compared for their
values
console.log(s === s); // true - ditto

console.log(n === o); // false - no implicit type conversion, types
are different
console.log(n === s); // false - types are different
console.log(o === s); // false - types are different
console.log(null === undefined); // false
console.log(o === null); // false
console.log(o === undefined); // false
```

You can use !== to handle the **Not Equal To** case while doing strict equality checks.

Weak equality using ==

Nothing should tempt you to use this form of equality. Seriously, stay away from this form. There are many bad things with this form of equality primarily due to the weak typing in JavaScript. The equality operator, ==, first tries to coerce the type before doing a comparison. The following examples show you how this works:

Condition	Output
`"" == "0"`	false
`0 == ""`	true
`0 == "0"`	true
`false == "false"`	false
`false == "0"`	true
`false == undefined`	false
`false == null`	false
`null == undefined`	true

From these examples, it's evident that weak equality can result in unexpected outcomes. Also, implicit type coercion is costly in terms of performance. So, in general, stay away from weak equality in JavaScript.

JavaScript types

We briefly discussed that JavaScript is a dynamic language. If you have a previous experience of strongly typed languages such as Java, you may feel a bit uncomfortable about the complete lack of type checks that you are used to. Purists argue that JavaScript should claim to have **tags** or perhaps **subtypes**, but not types. Though JavaScript does not have the traditional definition of **types**, it is absolutely essential to understand how JavaScript handles data types and coercion internally. Every nontrivial JavaScript program will need to handle value coercion in some form, so it's important that you understand the concept well.

Explicit coercion happens when you modify the type yourself. In the following example, you will convert a number to a String using the `toString()` method and extract the second character out of it:

```
var fortyTwo = 42;
console.log(fortyTwo.toString()[1]); //prints "2"
```

This is an example of an explicit type conversion. Again, we are using the word **type** loosely because type was not enforced anywhere when you declared the `fortyTwo` variable.

However, there are many different ways in which such coercion can happen. Coercion happening explicitly can be easy to understand and mostly reliable; but if you're not careful, coercion can happen in very strange and surprising ways.

Confusion around coercion is perhaps one of the most talked about frustrations for JavaScript developers. To make sure that you never have this confusion in your mind, let's revisit types in JavaScript. We talked about some concepts earlier:

```
typeof 1             === "number";    // true
typeof "1"           === "string";    // true
typeof { age: 39 }   === "object";    // true
typeof Symbol()      === "symbol";    // true
typeof undefined     === "undefined"; // true
typeof true          === "boolean";   // true
```

So far, so good. We already knew this and the examples that we just saw reinforce our ideas about types.

Conversion of a value from one type to another is called **casting** or explicit coercion. JavaScript also does implicit coercion by changing the type of a value based on certain guesses. These guesses make JavaScript work around several cases and unfortunately make it fail quietly and unexpectedly. The following snippet shows cases of explicit and implicit coercion:

```
var t=1;
var u=""+t; //implicit coercion
console.log(typeof t);  //"number"
console.log(typeof u);  //"string"
var v=String(t);  //Explicit coercion
console.log(typeof v);  //"string"
var x=null
console.log(""+x);  //"null"
```

It is easy to see what is happening here. When you use ""+t to a numeric value of t (1, in this case), JavaScript figures out that you are trying to concatenate *something* with a "" string. As only strings can be concatenated with other strings, JavaScript goes ahead and converts a numeric 1 to a "1" string and concatenates both into a resulting string value. This is what happens when JavaScript is asked to convert values implicitly. However, String(t) is a very deliberate call to convert a number to a String. This is an explicit conversion of types. The last bit is surprising. We are concatenating null with "" — shouldn't this fail?

So how does JavaScript do type conversions? How will an abstract value become a String or number or Boolean? JavaScript relies on toString(), toNumber(), and toBoolean() methods to do this internally.

When a non-String value is coerced into a String, JavaScript uses the `toString()` method internally to do this. All primitives have a natural string form—null has a string form of `"null"`, undefined has a string form of `"undefined"`, and so on. For Java developers, this is analogous to a class having a `toString()` method that returns a string representation of the class. We will see exactly how this works in case of objects.

So essentially you can do something similar to the following:

```
var a="abc";
console.log(a.length);
console.log(a.toUpperCase());
```

If you are keenly following and typing all these little snippets, you would have realized something strange in the previous snippet. How are we calling properties and methods on primitives? How come primitives have objects such as properties and methods? They don't.

As we discussed earlier, JavaScript kindly wraps these primitives in their wrappers by default thus making it possible for us to directly access the wrapper's methods and properties as if they were of the primitives themselves.

When any non-number value needs to be coerced into a number, JavaScript uses the `toNumber()` method internally: `true` becomes `1`, `undefined` becomes `NaN`, `false` becomes `0`, and `null` becomes `0`. The `toNumber()` method on strings works with literal conversion and if this fails, the method returns `NaN`.

What about some other cases?

```
typeof null ==="object" //true
```

Well, null is an object? Yes, an especially long-lasting bug makes this possible. Due to this bug, you need to be careful while testing if a value is null:

```
var x = null;
if (!x && typeof x === "object"){
  console.log("100% null");
}
```

What about other things that may have types, such as functions?

```
f = function test() {
  return 12;
}
console.log(typeof f === "function");  //prints "true"
```

What about arrays?

```
console.log (typeof [1,2,3,4]); //"object"
```

Sure enough, they are also objects. We will take a detailed look at functions and arrays later in the book.

In JavaScript, values have types, variables don't. Due to the dynamic nature of the language, variables can hold any value at any time.

JavaScript doesn't does not enforce types, which means that the language doesn't insist that a variable always hold values of the same initial type that it starts out with. A variable can hold a String, and in the next assignment, hold a number, and so on:

```
var a = 1;
typeof a; // "number"
a = false;
typeof a; // "boolean"
```

The `typeof` operator always returns a String:

```
typeof typeof 1; // "string"
```

Automatic semicolon insertion

Although JavaScript is based on the C style syntax, it does not enforce the use of semicolons in the source code.

However, JavaScript is not a semicolon-less language. A JavaScript language parser needs the semicolons in order to understand the source code. Therefore, the JavaScript parser automatically inserts them whenever it encounters a parse error due to a missing semicolon. It's important to note that **automatic semicolon insertion (ASI)** will only take effect in the presence of a newline (also known as a line break). Semicolons are not inserted in the middle of a line.

Basically, if the JavaScript parser parses a line where a parser error would occur (a missing expected ;) and it can insert one, it does so. What are the criteria to insert a semicolon? Only if there's nothing but white space and/or comments between the end of some statement and that line's newline/line break.

There have been raging debates on ASI—a feature justifiably considered to be a very bad design choice. There have been epic discussions on the Internet, such as https://github.com/twbs/bootstrap/issues/3057 and https://brendaneich. com/2012/04/the-infernal-semicolon/.

Before you judge the validity of these arguments, you need to understand what is affected by ASI. The following statements are affected by ASI:

- An empty statement
- A var statement
- An expression statement
- A do-while statement
- A continue statement
- A break statement
- A return statement
- A throw statement

The idea behind ASI is to make semicolons optional at the end of a line. This way, ASI helps the parser to determine when a statement ends. Normally, it ends with a semicolon. ASI dictates that a statement also ends in the following cases:

- A line terminator (for example, a newline) is followed by an illegal token
- A closing brace is encountered
- The end of the file has been reached

Let's see the following example:

```
if (a < 1) a = 1 console.log(a)
```

The `console` token is illegal after `1` and triggers ASI as follows:

```
if (a < 1) a = 1; console.log(a);
```

In the following code, the statement inside the braces is not terminated by a semicolon:

```
function add(a,b) { return a+b }
```

ASI creates a syntactically correct version of the preceding code:

```
function add(a,b) { return a+b; }
```

JavaScript style guide

Every programming language develops its own style and structure. Unfortunately, new developers don't put much effort in learning the stylistic nuances of a language. It is very difficult to develop this skill later once you have acquired bad practices. To produce beautiful, readable, and easily maintainable code, it is important to learn the correct style. There are a ton of style suggestions. We will be picking the most practical ones. Whenever applicable, we will discuss the appropriate style. Let's set some stylistic ground rules.

Whitespaces

Though whitespace is not important in JavaScript, the correct use of whitespace can make the code easy to read. The following guidelines will help in managing whitespaces in your code:

- Never mix spaces and tabs.
- Before you write any code, choose between soft indents (spaces) or real tabs. For readability, I always recommend that you set your editor's indent size to two characters—this means two spaces or two spaces representing a real tab.
- Always work with the *show invisibles* setting turned on. The benefits of this practice are as follows:
  - Enforced consistency.
  - Eliminates the end-of-line white spaces.
  - Eliminates blank line white spaces.
  - Commits and diffs that are easier to read.
  - Uses **EditorConfig** (http://editorconfig.org/) when possible.

Parentheses, line breaks, and braces

If, else, for, while, and try always have spaces and braces and span multiple lines. This style encourages readability. Let's see the following code:

```
//Cramped style (Bad)
if(condition) doSomeTask();

while(condition) i++;

for(var i=0;i<10;i++) iterate();

//Use whitespace for better readability (Good)
```

```
//Place 1 space before the leading brace.
if (condition) {
  // statements
}

while ( condition ) {
  // statements
}

for ( var i = 0; i < 100; i++ ) {
  // statements
}

// Better:

var i,
    length = 100;

for ( i = 0; i < length; i++ ) {
  // statements
}

// Or...

var i = 0,
    length = 100;

for ( ; i < length; i++ ) {
  // statements
}

var value;

for ( value in object ) {
  // statements
}


if ( true ) {
  // statements
} else {
  // statements
}
```

```
//Set off operators with spaces.
// bad
var x=y+5;

// good
var x = y + 5;

//End files with a single newline character.
// bad
(function(global) {
  // ...stuff...
})(this);

// bad
(function(global) {
  // ...stuff...
})(this);↵
↵

// good
(function(global) {
  // ...stuff...
})(this);↵
```

Quotes

Whether you prefer single or double quotes shouldn't matter; there is no difference in how JavaScript parses them. However, for the sake of consistency, never mix quotes in the same project. Pick one style and stick with it.

End of lines and empty lines

Whitespace can make it impossible to decipher code diffs and changelists. Many editors allow you to automatically remove extra empty lines and end of lines—you should use these.

Type checking

Checking the type of a variable can be done as follows:

```
//String:
typeof variable === "string"
//Number:
typeof variable === "number"
//Boolean:
typeof variable === "boolean"
//Object:
typeof variable === "object"
//null:
variable === null
//null or undefined:
variable == null
```

Type casting

Perform type coercion at the beginning of the statement as follows:

```
// bad
const totalScore = this.reviewScore + '';
// good
const totalScore = String(this.reviewScore);
```

Use `parseInt()` for Numbers and always with a radix for the type casting:

```
const inputValue = '4';
// bad
const val = new Number(inputValue);
// bad
const val = +inputValue;
// bad
const val = inputValue >> 0;
// bad
const val = parseInt(inputValue);
// good
const val = Number(inputValue);
// good
const val = parseInt(inputValue, 10);
```

The following example shows you how to type cast using Booleans:

```
const age = 0;  // bad
const hasAge = new Boolean(age);  // good
const hasAge = Boolean(age); // good
const hasAge = !!age;
```

Conditional evaluation

There are various stylistic guidelines around conditional statements. Let's study the following code:

```
// When evaluating that array has length,
// WRONG:
if ( array.length > 0 ) ...

// evaluate truthiness(GOOD):
if ( array.length ) ...

// When evaluating that an array is empty,
// (BAD):
if ( array.length === 0 ) ...

// evaluate truthiness(GOOD):
if ( !array.length ) ...

// When checking if string is not empty,
// (BAD):
if ( string !== "" ) ...

// evaluate truthiness (GOOD):
if ( string ) ...

// When checking if a string is empty,
// BAD:
if ( string === "" ) ...

// evaluate falsy-ness (GOOD):
if ( !string ) ...

// When checking if a reference is true,
// BAD:
if ( foo === true ) ...
```

```
// GOOD
if ( foo ) ...

// When checking if a reference is false,
// BAD:
if ( foo === false ) ...

// GOOD
if ( !foo ) ...

// this will also match: 0, "", null, undefined, NaN
// If you MUST test for a boolean false, then use
if ( foo === false ) ...

// a reference that might be null or undefined, but NOT false, "" or
0,
// BAD:
if ( foo === null || foo === undefined ) ...

// GOOD
if ( foo == null ) ...

// Don't complicate matters
return x === 0 ? 'sunday' : x === 1 ? 'Monday' : 'Tuesday';

// Better:
if (x === 0) {
    return 'Sunday';
} else if (x === 1) {
    return 'Monday';
} else {
    return 'Tuesday';
}

// Even Better:
switch (x) {
    case 0:
        return 'Sunday';
    case 1:
        return 'Monday';
    default:
        return 'Tuesday';
}
```

Naming

Naming is super important. I am sure that you have encountered code with terse and undecipherable naming. Let's study the following lines of code:

```javascript
//Avoid single letter names. Be descriptive with your naming.
// bad
function q() {

}

// good
function query() {
}

//Use camelCase when naming objects, functions, and instances.
// bad
const OBJEcT = {};
const this_is_object = {};
function c() {}

// good
const thisIsObject = {};
function thisIsFunction() {}

//Use PascalCase when naming constructors or classes.
// bad
function user(options) {
  this.name = options.name;
}

const bad = new user({
  name: 'nope',
});

// good
class User {
  constructor(options) {
    this.name = options.name;
  }
}
```

```
const good = new User({
  name: 'yup',
});

// Use a leading underscore _ when naming private properties.
// bad
this.__firstName__ = 'Panda';
this.firstName_ = 'Panda';

// good
this._firstName = 'Panda';
```

The eval() method is evil

The `eval()` method, which takes a String containing JavaScript code, compiles it and runs it, is one of the most misused methods in JavaScript. There are a few situations where you will find yourself using `eval()`, for example, when you are building an expression based on the user input.

However, most of the time, `eval()` is used is just because it gets the job done. The `eval()` method is too hacky and makes the code unpredictable. It's slow, unwieldy, and tends to magnify the damage when you make a mistake. If you are considering using `eval()`, then there is probably a better way.

The following snippet shows the usage of `eval()`:

```
console.log(typeof eval(new String("1+1")));  // "object"
console.log(eval(new String("1+1")));         //1+1
console.log(eval("1+1"));                     // 2
console.log(typeof eval("1+1"));              // returns "number"
var expression = new String("1+1");
console.log(eval(expression.toString()));     //2
```

I will refrain from showing other uses of `eval()` and make sure that you are discouraged enough to stay away from it.

The strict mode

ECMAScript 5 has a strict mode that results in cleaner JavaScript, with fewer unsafe features, more warnings, and more logical behavior. The normal (non-strict) mode is also called **sloppy mode**. The strict mode can help you avoid a few sloppy programming practices. If you are starting a new JavaScript project, I would highly recommend that you use the strict mode by default.

You switch on the strict mode by typing the following line first in your JavaScript file or in your `<script>` element:

```
'use strict';
```

Note that JavaScript engines that don't support ECMAScript 5 will simply ignore the preceding statement and continue as non-strict mode.

If you want to switch on the strict mode per function, you can do it as follows:

```
function foo() {
    'use strict';

}
```

This is handy when you are working with a legacy code base where switching on the strict mode everywhere may break things.

If you are working on an existing legacy code, be careful because using the strict mode can break things. There are caveats on this:

Enabling the strict mode for an existing code can break it

The code may rely on a feature that is not available anymore or on behavior that is different in a sloppy mode than in a strict mode. Don't forget that you have the option to add single strict mode functions to files that are in the sloppy mode.

Package with care

When you concatenate and/or minify files, you have to be careful that the strict mode isn't switched off where it should be switched on or vice versa. Both can break code.

The following sections explain the strict mode features in more detail. You normally don't need to know them as you will mostly get warnings for things that you shouldn't do anyway.

Variables must be declared in strict mode

All variables must be explicitly declared in strict mode. This helps to prevent typos. In the sloppy mode, assigning to an undeclared variable creates a global variable:

```
function sloppyFunc() {
  sloppyVar = 123;
} sloppyFunc();  // creates global variable `sloppyVar`
console.log(sloppyVar);  // 123
```

In the strict mode, assigning to an undeclared variable throws an exception:

```
function strictFunc() {
  'use strict';
  strictVar = 123;
}
strictFunc();  // ReferenceError: strictVar is not defined
```

The eval() function is cleaner in strict mode

In strict mode, the `eval()` function becomes less quirky: variables declared in the evaluated string are not added to the scope surrounding `eval()` anymore.

Features that are blocked in strict mode

The with statement is not allowed. (We will discuss this in the book later.) You get a syntax error at compile time (when loading the code).

In the sloppy mode, an integer with a leading zero is interpreted as octal (base 8) as follows:

```
> 010 === 8 true
```

In strict mode, you get a syntax error if you use this kind of literal:

```
function f() {
'use strict';
return 010
}
//SyntaxError: Octal literals are not allowed in
```

Running JSHint

JSHint is a program that flags suspicious usage in programs written in JavaScript. The core project consists of a library itself as well as a **command line interface (CLI)** program distributed as a Node module.

If you have Node.js installed, you can install JSHint using npm as follows:

```
npm install jshint -g
```

Once JSHint is installed, you can lint a single or multiple JavaScript files. Save the following JavaScript code snippet in the `test.js` file:

```
function f(condition) {
  switch (condition) {
  case 1:
    console.log(1);
  case 2:
    console.log(1);
  }
}
```

When we run the file using JSHint, it will warn us of a missing break statement in the switch case as follows:

```
>jshint test.js
test.js: line 4, col 19, Expected a 'break' statement before 'case'.
1 error
```

JSHint is configurable to suit your needs. Check the documentation at http:// jshint.com/docs/ to see how you can customize JSHint according to your project needs. I use JSHint extensively and suggest you start using it. You will be surprised to see how many hidden bugs and stylistic issues you will be able to fix in your code with such a simple tool.

You can run JSHint at the root of your project and lint the entire project. You can place JSHint directives in the .jshintrc file. This file may look something as follows:

```
{
    "asi": false,
    "expr": true,
    "loopfunc": true,
    "curly": false,
    "evil": true,
    "white": true,
    "undef": true,
    "indent": 4
}
```

Summary

In this chapter, we set some foundations around JavaScript grammar, types, and stylistic considerations. We have consciously not talked about other important aspects such as functions, variable scopes, and closures primarily because they deserve their own place in this book. I am sure that this chapter helps you understand some of the primary concepts of JavaScript. With these foundations in place, we will take a look at how we can write professional quality JavaScript code.

2

Functions, Closures, and Modules

In the previous chapter, we deliberately did not discuss certain aspects of JavaScript. These are some of the features of the language that give JavaScript its power and elegance. If you are an intermediate- or advanced-level JavaScript programmer, you may be actively using objects and functions. In many cases, however, developers stumble at these fundamental levels and develop a half-baked or sometimes wrong understanding of the core JavaScript constructs. There is generally a very poor understanding of the concept of closures in JavaScript, due to which many programmers cannot use the functional aspects of JavaScript very well. In JavaScript, there is a strong interconnection between objects, functions, and closures. Understanding the strong relationship between these three concepts can vastly improve our JavaScript programming ability, giving us a strong foundation for any type of application development.

Functions are fundamental to JavaScript. Understanding functions in JavaScript is the single most important weapon in your arsenal. The most important fact about functions is that in JavaScript, functions are first-class objects. They are treated like any other JavaScript object. Just like other JavaScript data types, they can be referenced by variables, declared with literals, and even passed as function parameters.

As with any other object in JavaScript, functions have the following capabilities:

- They can be created via literals
- They can be assigned to variables, array entries, and properties of other objects
- They can be passed as arguments to functions
- They can be returned as values from functions
- They can possess properties that can be dynamically created and assigned

We will talk about each of these unique abilities of a JavaScript function in this chapter and the rest of the book.

A function literal

One of the most important concepts in JavaScript is that the functions are the primary unit of execution. Functions are the pieces where you will wrap all your code, hence they will give your programs a structure.

JavaScript functions are declared using a function literal.

Function literals are composed of the following four parts:

- The function keyword.
- An optional name that, if specified, must be a valid JavaScript identifier.
- A list of parameter names enclosed in parentheses. If there are no parameters to the function, you need to provide empty parentheses.
- The body of the function as a series of JavaScript statements enclosed in braces.

A function declaration

The following is a very trivial example to demonstrate all the components of a function declaration:

```
function add(a,b){
  return a+b;
}
c = add(1,2);
console.log(c);  //prints 3
```

The declaration begins with a `function` keyword followed by the function name. The function name is optional. If a function is not given a name, it is said to be anonymous. We will see how anonymous functions are used. The third part is the set of parameters of the function, wrapped in parentheses. Within the parentheses is a set of zero or more parameter names separated by commas. These names will be defined as variables in the function, and instead of being initialized to undefined, they will be initialized to the arguments supplied when the function is invoked. The fourth part is a set of statements wrapped in curly braces. These statements are the body of the function. They are executed when the function is invoked.

This method of function declaration is also known as **function statement**. When you declare functions like this, the content of the function is compiled and an object with the same name as the function is created.

Another way of function declaration is via **function expressions**:

```
var add = function(a,b){
   return a+b;
}
c = add(1,2);
console.log(c);  //prints 3
```

Here, we are creating an anonymous function and assigning it to an `add` variable; this variable is used to invoke the function as in the earlier example. One problem with this style of function declaration is that we cannot have recursive calls to this kind of function. Recursion is an elegant style of coding where the function calls itself. You can use named function expressions to solve this limitation. As an example, refer to the following function to compute the factorial of a given number, n:

```
var facto = function factorial(n) {
   if (n <= 1)
      return 1;
   return n * factorial(n - 1);
};
console.log(facto(3));  //prints 6
```

Here, instead of creating an anonymous function, you are creating a named function. Now, because the function has a name, it can call itself recursively.

Finally, you can create self-invoking function expressions (we will discuss them later):

```
(function sayHello() {
   console.log("hello!");
})();
```

Once defined, a function can be called in other JavaScript functions. After the function body is executed, the caller code (that executed the function) continues to execute. You can also pass a function as a parameter to another function:

```
function changeCase(val) {
    return val.toUpperCase();
}
function demofunc(a, passfunction) {
    console.log(passfunction(a));
}
demofunc("smallcase", changeCase);
```

In the preceding example, we are calling the `demofunc()` function with two parameters. The first parameter is the string that we want to convert to uppercase and the second one is the function reference to the `changeCase()` function. In `demofunc()`, we call the `changeCase()` function via its reference passed to the `passfunction` argument. Here we are passing a function reference as an argument to another function. This powerful concept will be discussed in detail later in the book when we discuss callbacks.

A function may or may not return a value. In the previous examples, we saw that the add function returned a value to the calling code. Apart from returning a value at the end of the function, calling `return` explicitly allows you to conditionally return from a function:

```
var looper = function(x){
    if (x%5===0) {
        return;
    }
    console.log(x)
}
for(var i=1;i<10;i++){
    looper(i);
}
```

This code snippet prints 1, 2, 3, 4, 6, 7, 8, and 9, and not 5. When the `if (x%5===0)` condition is evaluated to true, the code simply returns from the function and the rest of the code is not executed.

Functions as data

In JavaScript, functions can be assigned to variables, and variables are data. You will shortly see that this is a powerful concept. Let's see the following example:

```
var say = console.log;
say("I can also say things");
```

In the preceding example, we assigned the familiar `console.log()` function to the say variable. Any function can be assigned to a variable as shown in the preceding example. Adding parentheses to the variable will invoke it. Moreover, you can pass functions in other functions as parameters. Study the following example carefully and type it in JS Bin:

```
var validateDataForAge = function(data) {
  person = data();
  console.log(person);
  if (person.age <1 || person.age > 99){
    return true;
  }else{
    return false;
  }
};

var errorHandlerForAge = function(error) {
  console.log("Error while processing age");
};

function parseRequest(data,validateData,errorHandler) {
  var error = validateData(data);
  if (!error) {
    console.log("no errors");
  } else {
    errorHandler();
  }
}

var generateDataForScientist = function() {
  return {
    name: "Albert Einstein",
    age : Math.floor(Math.random() * (100 - 1)) + 1,
  };
};
```

```
var generateDataForComposer = function() {
  return {
    name: "J S Bach",
    age : Math.floor(Math.random() * (100 - 1)) + 1,
  };
};

//parse request
parseRequest(generateDataForScientist, validateDataForAge,
errorHandlerForAge);
parseRequest(generateDataForComposer, validateDataForAge,
errorHandlerForAge);
```

In this example, we are passing functions as parameters to a `parseRequest()` function. We are passing different functions for two different calls, `generateDataForScientist` and `generateDataForComposers`, while the other two functions remain the same. You can observe that we defined a generic `parseRequest()`. It takes three functions as arguments, which are responsible for stitching together the specifics: the data, validator, and error handler. The `parseRequest()` function is fully extensible and customizable, and because it will be invoked by every request, there is a single, clean debugging point. I am sure that you have started to appreciate the incredible power that JavaScript functions provide.

Scoping

For beginners, JavaScript scoping is slightly confusing. These concepts may seem straightforward; however, they are not. Some important subtleties exist that must be understood in order to master the concept. So what is Scope? In JavaScript, scope refers to the current context of code.

A variable's scope is the context in which the variable exists. The scope specifies from where you can access a variable and whether you have access to the variable in that context. Scopes can be globally or locally defined.

Global scope

Any variable that you declare is by default defined in global scope. This is one of
the most annoying language design decisions taken in JavaScript. As a global
variable is visible in all other scopes, a global variable can be modified by any scope.
Global variables make it harder to run loosely coupled subprograms in the same
program/module. If the subprograms happen to have global variables that share
the same names, then they will interfere with each other and likely fail, usually
in difficult-to-diagnose ways. This is sometimes known as namespace clash.
We discussed global scope in the previous chapter but let's revisit it briefly to
understand how best to avoid this.

You can create a global variable in two ways:

* The first way is to place a var statement outside any function. Essentially,
  any variable declared outside a function is defined in the global scope.

* The second way is to omit the var statement while declaring a variable (also
  called implied globals). I think this was designed as a convenience for new
  programmers but turned out to be a nightmare. Even within a function
  scope, if you omit the var statement while declaring a variable, it's created
  by default in the global scope. This is nasty. You should always run your
  program against **ESLint** or **JSHint** to let them flag such violations. The
  following example shows how global scope behaves:

```
//Global Scope
var a = 1;
function scopeTest() {
  console.log(a);
}
scopeTest();  //prints 1
```

Here we are declaring a variable outside the function and in the global scope. This
variable is available in the scopeTest() function. If you assign a new value to a
global scope variable within a function scope (local), the original value in the global
scope is overwritten:

```
//Global Scope
var a = 1;
function scopeTest() {
  a = 2; //Overwrites global variable 2, you omit 'var'
  console.log(a);
}
console.log(a); //prints 1
scopeTest();  //prints 2
console.log(a); //prints 2 (global value is overwritten)
```

Local scope

Unlike most programming languages, JavaScript does not have block-level scope (variables scoped to surrounding curly brackets); instead, JavaScript has function-level scope. Variables declared within a function are local variables and are only accessible within that function or by functions inside that function:

```
var scope_name = "Global";
function showScopeName () {
  // local variable; only accessible in this function
  var scope_name = "Local";
  console.log (scope_name); // Local
}
console.log (scope_name);      //prints - Global
showScopeName();               //prints - Local
```

Function-level scope versus block-level scope

JavaScript variables are scoped at the function level. You can think of this as a small bubble getting created that prevents the variable to be visible from outside this bubble. A function creates such a bubble for variables declared inside the function. You can visualize the bubbles as follows:

```
-GLOBAL SCOPE----------------------------------------------|
var g =0;                                                  |
function foo(a) { ----------------------|                  |
    var b = 1;                          |                  |
    //code                              |                  |
    function bar() { ------|            |                  |
        // ...             |ScopeBar    | ScopeFoo         |
    }                 ------|            |                  |
    // code                             |                  |
    var c = 2;                          |                  |
}---------------------------------------|                  |
foo();   //WORKS                                           |
bar();   //FAILS                                           |
----------------------------------------------------------|
```

JavaScript uses scope chains to establish the scope for a given function. There is typically one global scope, and each function defined has its own nested scope. Any function defined within another function has a local scope that is linked to the outer function. *It's always the position in the source that defines the scope.* When resolving a variable, JavaScript starts at the innermost scope and searches outwards. With this, let's look at various scoping rules in JavaScript.

In the preceding crudely drawn visual, you can see that the foo() function is defined in the global scope. The foo() function has its local scope and access to the g variable because it's in the global scope. The a, b, and c variables are available in the local scope because they are defined within the function scope. The bar() function is also declared within the function scope and is available within the foo() function. However, once the function scope is over, the bar() function is not available. You cannot see or call the bar() function from outside the foo() function—a scope bubble.

Now that the bar() function also has its own function scope (bubble), what is available in here? The bar() function has access to the foo() function and all the variables created in the parent scope of the foo() function—a, b, and c. The bar() function also has access to the global scoped variable, g.

This is a powerful idea. Take a moment to think about it. We just discussed how rampant and uncontrolled global scope can get in JavaScript. How about we take an arbitrary piece of code and wrap it around with a function? We will be able to hide and create a scope bubble around this piece of code. Creating the correct scope using function wrapping will help us create correct code and prevent difficult-to-detect bugs.

Another advantage of the function scope and hiding variables and functions within this scope is that you can avoid collisions between two identifiers. The following example shows such a bad case:

```
function foo() {
  function bar(a) {
    i = 2; // changing the 'i' in the enclosing scope's for-loop
    console.log(a+i);
  }
  for (var i=0; i<10; i++) {
    bar(i); // infinite loop
  }
}
foo();
```

In the `bar()` function, we are inadvertently modifying the value of `i=2`. When we call `bar()` from within the `for` loop, the value of the `i` variable is set to `2` and we never come out of an infinite loop. This is a bad case of namespace collision.

So far, using functions as a scope sounds like a great way to achieve modularity and correctness in JavaScript. Well, though this technique works, it's not really ideal. The first problem is that we must create a named function. If we keep creating such functions just to introduce the function scope, we pollute the global scope or parent scope. Additionally, we have to keep calling such functions. This introduces a lot of boilerplate, which makes the code unreadable over time:

```
var a = 1;
//Lets introduce a function -scope
//1. Add a named function foo() into the global scope
function foo() {
  var a = 2;
  console.log( a ); // 2
}
//2. Now call the named function foo()
foo();
console.log( a ); // 1
```

We introduced the function scope by creating a new function `foo()` to the global scope and called this function later to execute the code.

In JavaScript, you can solve both these problems by creating functions that immediately get executed. Carefully study and type the following example:

```
var a = 1;
//Lets introduce a function -scope
//1. Add a named function foo() into the global scope
(function foo() {
    var a = 2;
    console.log( a ); // 2
})(); //<---this function executes immediately
console.log( a ); // 1
```

Notice that the wrapping function statement starts with `function`. This means that instead of treating the function as a standard declaration, the function is treated as a function expression.

The `(function foo(){     })` statement as an expression means that the identifier `foo` is found only in the scope of the `foo()` function, not in the outer scope. Hiding the name `foo` in itself means that it does not pollute the enclosing scope unnecessarily. This is so useful and far better. We add `()` after the function expression to execute it immediately. So the complete pattern looks as follows:

```
(function foo(){ /* code */ })();
```

This pattern is so common that it has a name: **IIFE**, which stands for **Immediately Invoked Function Expression**. Several programmers omit the function name when they use IIFE. As the primary use of IIFE is to introduce function-level scope, naming the function is not really required. We can write the earlier example as follows:

```
var a = 1;
(function() {
    var a = 2;
    console.log( a ); // 2
})();
console.log( a ); // 1
```

Here we are creating an anonymous function as IIFE. While this is identical to the earlier named IIFE, there are a few drawbacks of using anonymous IIFEs:

- As you can't see the function name in the stack traces, debugging such code is very difficult
- You cannot use recursion on anonymous functions (as we discussed earlier)
- Overusing anonymous IIFEs sometimes results in unreadable code

Douglas Crockford and a few other experts recommend a slight variation of IIFE:

```
(function(){ /* code */ }());
```

Both these IIFE forms are popular and you will see a lot of code using both these variations.

You can pass parameters to IIFEs. The following example shows you how to pass parameters to IIFEs:

```
(function foo(b) {
    var a = 2;
    console.log( a + b );
})(3); //prints 5
```

Inline function expressions

There is another popular usage of inline function expressions where the functions are passed as parameters to other functions:

```javascript
function setActiveTab(activeTabHandler, tab){
  //set active tab
  //call handler
  activeTabHandler();
}
setActiveTab( function (){
  console.log( "Setting active tab" );
}, 1 );
//prints "Setting active tab"
```

Again, you can name this inline function expression to make sure that you get a correct stack trace while you are debugging the code.

Block scopes

As we discussed earlier, JavaScript does not have the concept of block scopes. Programmers familiar with other languages such as Java or C find this very uncomfortable. **ECMAScript 6 (ES6)** introduces the **let** keyword to introduce traditional block scope. This is so incredibly convenient that if you are sure your environment is going to support ES6, you should always use the `let` keyword. See the following code:

```javascript
var foo = true;
if (foo) {
  let bar = 42; //variable bar is local in this block { }
  console.log( bar );
}
console.log( bar ); // ReferenceError
```

However, as things stand today, ES6 is not supported by default in most popular browsers.

This chapter so far should have given you a fair understanding of how scoping works in JavaScript. If you are still unclear, I would suggest that you stop here and revisit the earlier sections of this chapter. Research your doubts on the Internet or put your questions on Stack Overflow. In short, make sure that you have no doubts related to the scoping rules.

It is very natural for us to think of code execution happening from top to bottom, line by line. This is how most of JavaScript code is executed but with some exceptions.

Consider the following code:

```
console.log( a );
var a = 1;
```

If you said this is an invalid code and will result in undefined when we call console.log(), you are absolutely correct. However, what about this?

```
a = 1;
var a;
console.log( a );
```

What should be the output of the preceding code? It is natural to expect undefined as the var a statement comes after a = 1, and it would seem natural to assume that the variable is redefined and thus assigned the default undefined. However, the output will be 1.

When you see var a = 1, JavaScript splits it into two statements: var a and a = 1. The first statement, the declaration, is processed during the compilation phase. The second statement, the assignment, is left in place for the execution phase.

So the preceding snippet would actually be executed as follows:

```
var a;    //----Compilation phase

a = 1;    //------execution phase
console.log( a );
```

The first snippet is actually executed as follows:

```
var a;      //-----Compilation phase

console.log( a );
a = 1;      //------execution phase
```

So, as we can see, variable and function declarations are moved up to the top of the code during compilation phase—this is also popularly known as **hoisting**. It is very important to remember that only the declarations themselves are hoisted, while any assignments or other executable logic are left in place. The following snippet shows you how function declarations are hoisted:

```
foo();
function foo() {
    console.log(a); // undefined
    var a = 1;
}
```

The declaration of the `foo()` function is hoisted such that we are able to execute the function before defining it. One important aspect of hoisting is that it works per scope. Within the `foo()` function, declaration of the a variable will be hoisted to the top of the `foo()` function, and not to the top of the program. The actual execution of the `foo()` function with hoisting will be something as follows:

```
function foo() {
  var a;
  console.log(a); // undefined
  a = 1;
}
```

We saw that function declarations are hoisted but function expressions are not. The next section explains this case.

Function declarations versus function expressions

We saw two ways by which functions are defined. Though they both serve identical purposes, there is a difference between these two types of declarations. Check the following example:

```
//Function expression
functionOne();
//Error
//"TypeError: functionOne is not a function

var functionOne = function() {
  console.log("functionOne");
};
//Function declaration
functionTwo();
//No error
//Prints - functionTwo

function functionTwo() {
  console.log("functionTwo");
}
```

A function declaration is processed when execution enters the context in which it appears before any step-by-step code is executed. The function that it creates is given a proper name (`functionTwo()` in the preceding example) and this name is put in the scope in which the declaration appears. As it's processed before any step-by-step code in the same context, calling `functionTwo()` before defining it works without an error.

However, `functionOne()` is an anonymous function expression, evaluated when it's reached in the step-by-step execution of the code (also called runtime execution); we have to declare it before we can invoke it.

So essentially, the function declaration of `functionTwo()` was hoisted while the function expression of `functionOne()` was executed when line-by-line execution encountered it.

 Both function declarations and variable declarations are hoisted but functions are hoisted first, and then variables.

One thing to remember is that you should never use function declarations conditionally. This behavior is non-standardized and can behave differently across platforms. The following example shows such a snippet where we try to use function declarations conditionally. We are trying to assign different function body to function `sayMoo()` but such a conditional code is not guaranteed to work across all browsers and can result in unpredictable results:

```
// Never do this - different browsers will behave differently
if (true) {
  function sayMoo() {
    return 'trueMoo';
  }
}
else {
  function sayMoo() {
    return 'falseMoo';
  }
}
foo();
```

However, it's perfectly safe and, in fact, smart to do the same with function expressions:

```
var sayMoo;
if (true) {
  sayMoo = function() {
```

```
      return 'trueMoo';
    };
  }
  else {
    sayMoo = function() {
      return 'falseMoo';
    };
  }
  foo();
```

If you are curious to know why you should not use function declarations in conditional blocks, read on; otherwise, you can skip the following paragraph.

Function declarations are allowed to appear only in the program or function body. They cannot appear in a block ({ ... }). Blocks can only contain statements and not function declarations. Due to this, almost all implementations of JavaScript have behavior different from this. It is always advisable to *never* use function declarations in a conditional block.

Function expressions, on the other hand, are very popular. A very common pattern among JavaScript programmers is to fork function definitions based on some kind of a condition. As such forks usually happen in the same scope, it is almost always necessary to use function expressions.

The arguments parameter

The arguments parameter is a collection of all the arguments passed to the function. The collection has a property named `length` that contains the count of arguments, and the individual argument values can be obtained using an array indexing notation. Okay, we lied a bit. The arguments parameter is not a JavaScript array, and if you try to use array methods on arguments, you'll fail miserably. You can think of arguments as an array-like structure. This makes it possible to write functions that take an unspecified number of parameters. The following snippet shows you how you can pass a variable number of arguments to the function and iterate through them using an arguments array:

```
var sum = function () {
  var i, total = 0;
  for (i = 0; i < arguments.length; i += 1) {
    total += arguments[i];
  }
  return total;
};
console.log(sum(1,2,3,4,5,6,7,8,9)); // prints 45
console.log(sum(1,2,3,4,5)); // prints 15
```

As we discussed, the arguments parameter is not really an array; it is possible to convert it to an array as follows:

```
var args = Array.prototype.slice.call(arguments);
```

Once converted to an array, you can manipulate the list as you wish.

The this parameter

Whenever a function is invoked, in addition to the parameters that represent the explicit arguments that were provided on the function call, an implicit parameter named `this` is also passed to the function. It refers to an object that's implicitly associated with the function invocation, termed as a **function context**. If you have coded in Java, the `this` keyword will be familiar to you; like Java, `this` points to an instance of the class in which the method is defined.

Equipped with this knowledge, let's talk about various invocation methods.

Invocation as a function

If a function is not invoked as a method, constructor, or via `apply()` or `call()`, it's simply invoked *as a function*:

```
function add() {}
add();
var substract = function() {

};
substract();
```

When a function is invoked with this pattern, `this` is bound to the global object. Many experts believe this to be a bad design choice. It is natural to assume that `this` would be bound to the parent context. When you are in a situation such as this, you can capture the value of `this` in another variable. We will focus on this pattern later.

Invocation as a method

A method is a function tied to a property on an object. For methods, `this` is bound to the object on invocation:

```
var person = {
  name: 'Albert Einstein',
  age: 66,
  greet: function () {
```

```
      console.log(this.name);
    }
};
person.greet();
```

In this example, `this` is bound to the person object on invoking `greet` because `greet` is a method of person. Let's see how this behaves in both these invocation patterns.

Let's prepare this HTML and JavaScript harness:

```html
<!DOCTYPE html>
<html>
<head>
  <meta charset="utf-8">
  <title>This test</title>
  <script type="text/javascript">
    function testF(){ return this; }
    console.log(testF());
    var testFCopy = testF;
    console.log(testFCopy());
    var testObj = {
      testObjFunc: testF
    };
    console.log(testObj.testObjFunc ());
  </script>
</head>
<body>
</body>
</html>
```

In the **Firebug** console, you can see the following output:

The first two method invocations were invocation as a function; hence, the `this` parameter pointed to the global context (`Window`, in this case).

Next, we define an object with a `testObj` variable with a property named `testObjFunc` that receives a reference to `testF()` —don't fret if you are not really aware of object creation yet. By doing this, we created a `testObjMethod()` method. Now, when we invoke this method, we expect the function context to be displayed when we display the value of `this`.

Invocation as a constructor

Constructor functions are declared just like any other functions and there's nothing special about a function that's going to be used as a constructor. However, the way in which they are invoked is very different.

To invoke the function as a constructor, we precede the function invocation with the **new** keyword. When this happens, `this` is bound to the new object.

Before we discuss more, let's take a quick introduction to object orientation in JavaScript. We will, of course, discuss the topic in great detail in the next chapter. JavaScript is a prototypal inheritance language. This means that objects can inherit properties directly from other objects. The language is class-free. Functions that are designed to be called with the `new` prefix are called constructors. Usually, they are named using **PascalCase** as opposed to **CamelCase** for easier distinction. In the following example, notice that the `greet` function uses this to access the `name` property. The `this` parameter is bound to `Person`:

```
var Person = function (name) {
  this.name = name;
};
Person.prototype.greet = function () {
  return this.name;
};
var albert = new Person('Albert Einstein');
console.log(albert.greet());
```

We will discuss this particular invocation method when we study objects in the next chapter.

Invocation using apply() and call() methods

We said earlier that JavaScript functions are objects. Like other objects, they also have certain methods. To invoke a function using its `apply()` method, we pass two parameters to `apply()`: the object to be used as the function context and an array of values to be used as the invocation arguments. The `call()` method is used in a similar manner, except that the arguments are passed directly in the argument list rather than as an array.

Anonymous functions

We introduced you to anonymous functions a bit earlier in this chapter, and as they're a crucial concept, we will take a detailed look at them. For a language inspired by Scheme, anonymous functions are an important logical and structural construct.

Anonymous functions are typically used in cases where the function doesn't need to have a name for later reference. Let's look at some of the most popular usages of anonymous functions.

Anonymous functions while creating an object

An anonymous function can be assigned to an object property. When we do that, we can call that function with a dot (.) operator. If you are coming from a Java or other OO language background, you will find this very familiar. In such languages, a function, which is part of a class is generally called with a notation — Class. function(). Let's consider the following example:

```
var santa = {
  say :function(){
    console.log("ho ho ho");
  }
}
santa.say();
```

In this example, we are creating an object with a say property, which is an anonymous function. In this particular case, this property is known as a method and not a function. We don't need to name this function because we are going to invoke it as the object property. This is a popular pattern and should come in handy.

Anonymous functions while creating a list

Here, we are creating two anonymous functions and adding them to an array. (We will take a detailed look at arrays later.) Then, you loop through this array and execute the functions in a loop:

```
<script type="text/javascript">
var things = [
  function() { alert("ThingOne") },
  function() { alert("ThingTwo") },
];
for(var x=0; x<things.length; x++) {
  things[x]();
}
</script>
```

Anonymous functions as a parameter to another function

This is one of the most popular patterns and you will find such code in most professional libraries:

```
// function statement
function eventHandler(event){
  event();
}


eventHandler(function(){
  //do a lot of event related things
  console.log("Event fired");
});
```

You are passing the anonymous function to another function. In the receiving function, you are executing the function passed as a parameter. This can be very convenient if you are creating single-use functions such as object methods or event handlers. The anonymous function syntax is more concise than declaring a function and then doing something with it as two separate steps.

Anonymous functions in conditional logic

You can use anonymous function expressions to conditionally change behavior. The following example shows this pattern:

```
var shape;
if(shape_name === "SQUARE") {
  shape = function() {
    return "drawing square";
  }
}
else {
  shape = function() {
    return "drawing square";
  }
}
alert(shape());
```

Here, based on a condition, we are assigning a different implementation to the shape variable. This pattern can be very useful if used with care. Overusing this can result in unreadable and difficult-to-debug code.

Later in this book, we will look at several functional tricks such as **memoization** and caching function calls. If you have reached here by quickly reading through the entire chapter, I would suggest that you stop for a while and contemplate on what we have discussed so far. The last few pages contain a ton of information and it will take some time for all this information to sink in. I would suggest that you reread this chapter before proceeding further. The next section will focus on closures and the module pattern.

Closures

Traditionally, closures have been a feature of purely functional programming languages. JavaScript shows its affinity with such functional programming languages by considering closures integral to the core language constructs. Closures are gaining popularity in mainstream JavaScript libraries and advanced production code because they let you simplify complex operations. You will hear experienced JavaScript programmers talking almost reverently about closures—as if they are some magical construct far beyond the reach of the intellect that common men possess. However, this is not so. When you study this concept, you will find closures to be very obvious, almost matter-of-fact. Till you reach closure enlightenment, I suggest you read and reread this chapter, research on the Internet, write code, and read JavaScript libraries to understand how closures behave—but do not give up.

The first realization that you must have is that closure is everywhere in JavaScript. It is not a hidden special part of the language.

Before we jump into the nitty-gritty, let's quickly refresh the lexical scope in JavaScript. We discussed in great detail how lexical scope is determined at the function level in JavaScript. Lexical scope essentially determines where and how all identifiers are declared and predicts how they will be looked up during execution.

In a nutshell, closure is the scope created when a function is declared that allows the function to access and manipulate variables that are external to this function. In other words, closures allow a function to access all the variables, as well as other functions, that are in scope when the function itself is declared.

Let's look at some example code to understand this definition:

```
var outer = 'I am outer'; //Define a value in global scope
function outerFn() { //Declare a a function in global scope
  console.log(outer);
}
outerFn(); //prints - I am outer
```

Were you expecting something shiny? No, this is really the most ordinary case of a closure. We are declaring a variable in the global scope and declaring a function in the global scope. In the function, we are able to access the variable declared in the global scope — outer. So essentially, the outer scope for the outerFn() function is a closure and always available to outerFn(). This is a good start but perhaps then you are not sure why this is such a great thing.

Let's make things a bit more complex:

```
var outer = 'Outer'; //Variable declared in global scope
var copy;
function outerFn(){  //Function declared in global scope

  var inner = 'Inner'; //Variable has function scope only, can not be
  //accessed from outside

  function innerFn(){     //Inner function within Outer function,
    //both global context and outer
    //context are available hence can access
    //'outer' and 'inner'
    console.log(outer);
    console.log(inner);
  }
  copy=innerFn;          //Store reference to inner function,
  //because 'copy' itself is declared
  //in global context, it will be available
  //outside also
}
outerFn();
copy();  //Cant invoke innerFn() directly but can invoke via a
//variable declared in global scope
```

Let's analyze the preceding example. In innerFn(), the outer variable is available as it's part of the global context. We're executing the inner function after the outer function has been executed via copying a reference to the function to a global reference variable, copy. When innerFn() executes, the scope in outerFn() is gone and not visible at the point at which we're invoking the function through the copy variable. So shouldn't the following line fail?

```
console.log(inner);
```

Should the `inner` variable be undefined? However, the output of the preceding code snippet is as follows:

```
"Outer"
"Inner"
```

What phenomenon allows the `inner` variable to still be available when we execute the inner function, long after the scope in which it was created has gone away? When we declared `innerFn()` in `outerFn()`, not only was the function declaration defined, but a closure was also created that encompasses not only the function declaration, but also all the variables that are in scope at the point of the declaration. When `innerFn()` executes, even if it's executed after the scope in which it was declared goes away, it has access to the original scope in which it was declared through its closure.

Let's continue to expand this example to understand how far you can go with closures:

```
var outer='outer';
var copy;
function outerFn() {
  var inner='inner';
  function innerFn(param){
    console.log(outer);
    console.log(inner);
    console.log(param);
    console.log(magic);
  }
  copy=innerFn;
}
console.log(magic); //ERROR: magic not defined
var magic="Magic";
outerFn();
copy("copy");
```

In the preceding example, we have added a few more things. First, we added a parameter to `innerFn()` — just to illustrate that parameters are also part of the closure. There are two important points that we want to highlight.

All variables in an outer scope are included even if they are declared after the function is declared. This makes it possible for the line, `console.log(magic)`, in `innerFn()`, to work.

However, the same line, `console.log(magic)`, in the global scope will fail because even within the same scope, variables not yet defined cannot be referenced.

All these examples were intended to convey a few concepts that govern how closures work. Closures are a prominent feature in the JavaScript language and you can see them in most libraries.

Let's look at some popular patterns around closures.

Timers and callbacks

In implementing timers or callbacks, you need to call the handler asynchronously, mostly at a later point in time. Due to the asynchronous calls, we need to access variables from outside the scope in such functions. Consider the following example:

```
function delay(message) {
  setTimeout( function timerFn(){
    console.log( message );
  }, 1000 );
}
delay( "Hello World" );
```

We pass the inner `timerFn()` function to the built-in library function, `setTimeout()`. However, `timerFn()` has a scope closure over the scope of `delay()`, and hence it can reference the variable message.

Private variables

Closures are frequently used to encapsulate some information as private variables. JavaScript does not allow such encapsulation found in programming languages such as Java or C++, but by using closures, we can achieve similar encapsulation:

```
function privateTest(){
  var points=0;
  this.getPoints=function(){
    return points;
  };
  this.score=function(){
    points++;
  };
}

var private = new privateTest();
private.score();
console.log(private.points); // undefined
console.log(private.getPoints());
```

In the preceding example, we are creating a function that we intend to call as a constructor. In this `privateTest()` function, we are creating a `var points=0` variable as a function-scoped variable. This variable is available only in `privateTest()`. Additionally, we create an accessor function (also called a getter) — `getPoints()` — this method allows us to read the value of only the points variable from outside `privateTest()`, making this variable private to the function. However, another method, `score()`, allows us to modify the value of the private point variable without directly accessing it from outside. This makes it possible for us to write code where a private variable is updated in a controlled fashion. This pattern can be very useful when you are writing libraries where you want to control how variables are accessed based on a contract and pre-established interface.

Loops and closures

Consider the following example of using functions inside loops:

```
for (var i=1; i<=5; i++) {
  setTimeout( function delay(){
    console.log( i );
  }, i*100);
}
```

This snippet should print 1, 2, 3, 4, and 5 on the console at an interval of 100 ms, right? Instead, it prints 6, 6, 6, 6, and 6 at an interval of 100 ms. Why is this happening? Here, we encounter a common issue with closures and looping. The i variable is being updated after the function is bound. This means that every bound function handler will always print the last value stored in i. In fact, the timeout function callbacks are running after the completion of the loop. This is such a common problem that JSLint will warn you if you try to use functions this way inside a loop.

How can we fix this behavior? We can introduce a function scope and local copy of the i variable in that scope. The following snippet shows you how we can do this:

```
for (var i=1; i<=5; i++) {
  (function(j){
    setTimeout( function delay(){
      console.log( j );
    }, j*100);
  })( i );
}
```

We pass the `i` variable and copy it to the `j` variable local to the IIFE. The introduction of an IIFE inside each iteration creates a new scope for each iteration and hence updates the local copy with the correct value.

Modules

Modules are used to mimic classes and focus on public and private access to variables and functions. Modules help in reducing the global scope pollution. Effective use of modules can reduce name collisions across a large code base. A typical format that this pattern takes is as follows:

```
Var moduleName=function() {
  //private state
  //private functions
  return {
     //public state
     //public variables
  }
}
```

There are two requirements to implement this pattern in the preceding format:

* There must be an outer enclosing function that needs to be executed at least once.

* This enclosing function must return at least one inner function. This is necessary to create a closure over the private state—without this, you can't access the private state at all.

Check the following example of a module:

```
var superModule = (function (){
  var secret = 'supersecretkey';
  var passcode = 'nuke';

  function getSecret() {
    console.log( secret );
  }

  function getPassCode() {
    console.log( passcode );
  }
```

```
    return {
      getSecret: getSecret,
      getPassCode: getPassCode
    };
  })();
superModule.getSecret();
superModule.getPassCode();
```

This example satisfies both the conditions. Firstly, we create an IIFE or a named function to act as an outer enclosure. The variables defined will remain private because they are scoped in the function. We return the public functions to make sure that we have a closure over the private scope. Using IIFE in the module pattern will actually result in a singleton instance of this function. If you want to create multiple instances, you can create named function expressions as part of the module as well.

We will keep exploring various facets of functional aspects of JavaScript and closures in particular. There can be a lot of imaginative uses of such elegant constructs. An effective way to understand various patterns is to study the code of popular libraries and practice writing these patterns in your code.

Stylistic considerations

As in the previous chapter, we will conclude this discussion with certain stylistic considerations. Again, these are generally accepted guidelines and not rules — feel free to deviate from them if you have reason to believe otherwise:

- Use function declarations instead of function expressions:

```
// bad
const foo = function () {
};

// good
function foo() {
}
```

- Never declare a function in a non-function block (if, while, and so on). Assign the function to a variable instead. Browsers allow you to do it, but they all interpret it differently.

- Never name a parameter `arguments`. This will take precedence over the `arguments` object that is given to every function scope.

Summary

In this chapter, we studied JavaScript functions. In JavaScript, functions play a critical role. We discussed how functions are created and used. We also discussed important ideas of closures and the scope of variables in terms of functions. We discussed functions as a way to create visibility classes and encapsulation.

In the next chapter, we will look at various data structures and data manipulation techniques in JavaScript.

3
Data Structures and Manipulation

Most of the time that you spend in programming, you do something to manipulate data. You process properties of data, derive conclusions based on the data, and change the nature of the data. In this chapter, we will take an exhaustive look at various data structures and data manipulation techniques in JavaScript. With the correct usage of these expressive constructs, your programs will be correct, concise, easy to read, and most probably faster. This will be explained with the help of the following topics:

- Regular expressions
- Exact match
- Match from a class of characters
- Repeated occurrences
- Beginning and end
- Backreferences
- Greedy and lazy quantifiers
- Arrays
- Maps
- Sets
- A matter of style

Regular expressions

If you are not familiar with regular expressions, I request you to spend time learning them. Learning and using regular expressions effectively is one of the most rewarding skills that you will gain. During most of the code review sessions, the first thing that I comment on is how a piece of code can be converted to a single line of **regular expression** (or **RegEx**). If you study popular JavaScript libraries, you will be surprised to see how ubiquitous RegEx are. Most seasoned engineers rely on RegEx primarily because once you know how to use them, they are concise and easy to test. However, learning RegEx will take a significant amount of effort and time. A regular expression is a way to express a pattern to match strings of text. The expression itself consists of terms and operators that allow us to define these patterns. We'll see what these terms and operators consist of shortly.

In JavaScript, there are two ways to create a regular expression: via a regular expression literal and constructing an instance of a `RegExp` object.

For example, if we wanted to create a RegEx that matches the string test exactly, we could use the following RegEx literal:

```
var pattern = /test/;
```

RegEx literals are delimited using forward slashes. Alternatively, we could construct a `RegExp` instance, passing the RegEx as a string:

```
var pattern = new RegExp("test");
```

Both of these formats result in the same RegEx being created in the variable pattern. In addition to the expression itself, there are three flags that can be associated with a RegEx:

- `i`: This makes the RegEx case-insensitive, so `/test/i` matches not only test, but also Test, TEST, tEsT, and so on.
- `g`: This matches all the instances of the pattern as opposed to the default of local, which matches the first occurrence only. More on this later.
- `m`: This allows matches across multiple lines that might be obtained from the value of a `textarea` element.

These flags are appended to the end of the literal (for example, `/test/ig`) or passed in a string as the second parameter to the `RegExp` constructor (`new RegExp("test", "ig")`).

The following example illustrates the various flags and how they affect the pattern match:

```
var pattern = /orange/;
console.log(pattern.test("orange")); // true

var patternIgnoreCase = /orange/i;
console.log(patternIgnoreCase.test("Orange")); // true

var patternGlobal = /orange/ig;
console.log(patternGlobal.test("Orange Juice")); // true
```

It isn't very exciting if we can just test whether the pattern matches a string. Let's see how we can express more complex patterns.

Exact match

Any sequence of characters that's not a special RegEx character or operator represents a character literal:

```
var pattern = /orange/;
```

We mean o followed by r followed by a followed by n followed by ... — you get the point. We rarely use exact match when using RegEx because that is the same as comparing two strings. Exact match patterns are sometimes called simple patterns.

Match from a class of characters

If you want to match against a set of characters, you can place the set inside []. For example, [abc] would mean any character a, b, or c:

```
var pattern = /[abc]/;
console.log(pattern.test('a')); //true
console.log(pattern.test('d')); //false
```

You can specify that you want to match anything but the pattern by adding a ^ (caret sign) at the beginning of the pattern:

```
var pattern = /[^abc]/;
console.log(pattern.test('a')); //false
console.log(pattern.test('d')); //true
```

One critical variation of this pattern is a range of values. If we want to match against a sequential range of characters or numbers, we can use the following pattern:

```
var pattern = /[0-5]/;
console.log(pattern.test(3)); //true
console.log(pattern.test(12345)); //true
console.log(pattern.test(9)); //false
console.log(pattern.test(6789)); //false
console.log(/[0123456789]/.test("This is year 2015")); //true
```

Special characters such as $ and period (.) characters either represent matches to something other than themselves or operators that qualify the preceding term. In fact, we've already seen how [,], -, and ^ characters are used to represent something other than their literal values.

How do we specify that we want to match a literal [or $ or ^ or some other special character? Within a RegEx, the backslash character escapes whatever character follows it, making it a literal match term. So \[specifies a literal match to the [character rather than the opening of a character class expression. A double backslash (\\) matches a single backslash.

In the preceding examples, we saw the test() method that returns **true** or **false** based on the pattern matched. There are times when you want to access occurrences of a particular pattern. The exec() method comes in handy in such situations.

The exec() method takes a string as an argument and returns an array containing all matches. Consider the following example:

```
var strToMatch = 'A Toyota! Race fast, safe car! A Toyota!';
var regExAt = /Toy/;
var arrMatches = regExAt.exec(strToMatch);
console.log(arrMatches);
```

The output of this snippet would be **['Toy']**; if you want all the instances of the pattern Toy, you can use the g (global) flag as follows:

```
var strToMatch = 'A Toyota! Race fast, safe car! A Toyota!';
var regExAt = /Toy/g;
var arrMatches = regExAt.exec(strToMatch);
console.log(arrMatches);
```

This will return all the occurrences of the word `oyo` from the original text. The String object contains the `match()` method that has similar functionality of the `exec()` method. The `match()` method is called on a String object and the RegEx is passed to it as a parameter. Consider the following example:

```
var strToMatch = 'A Toyota! Race fast, safe car! A Toyota!';
var regExAt = /Toy/;
var arrMatches = strToMatch.match(regExAt);
console.log(arrMatches);
```

In this example, we are calling the `match()` method on the String object. We pass the RegEx as a parameter to the `match()` method. The results are the same in both these cases.

The other String object method is `replace()`. It replaces all the occurrences of a substring with a different string:

```
var strToMatch = 'Blue is your favorite color ?';
var regExAt = /Blue/;
console.log(strToMatch.replace(regExAt, "Red"));
//Output- "Red is your favorite color ?"
```

It is possible to pass a function as a second parameter of the `replace()` method. The `replace()` function takes the matching text as a parameter and returns the text that is used as a replacement:

```
var strToMatch = 'Blue is your favorite color ?';
var regExAt = /Blue/;
console.log(strToMatch.replace(regExAt, function(matchingText){
  return 'Red';
}));
//Output- "Red is your favorite color ?"
```

The String object's `split()` method also takes a RegEx parameter and returns an array containing all the substrings generated after splitting the original string:

```
var sColor = 'sun,moon,stars';
var reComma = /\,/;
console.log(sColor.split(reComma));
//Output - ["sun", "moon", "stars"]
```

We need to add a backslash before the comma because a comma is treated specially in RegEx and we need to escape it if we want to use it literally.

Using simple character classes, you can match multiple patterns. For example, if you want to match cat, bat, and fat, the following snippet shows you how to use simple character classes:

```
var strToMatch = 'wooden bat, smelly Cat,a fat cat';
var re = /[bcf]at/gi;
var arrMatches = strToMatch.match(re);
console.log(arrMatches);
//["bat", "Cat", "fat", "cat"]
```

As you can see, this variation opens up possibilities to write concise RegEx patterns. Take the following example:

```
var strToMatch = 'i1,i2,i3,i4,i5,i6,i7,i8,i9';
var re = /i[0-5]/gi;
var arrMatches = strToMatch.match(re);
console.log(arrMatches);
//["i1", "i2", "i3", "i4", "i5"]
```

In this example, we are matching the numeric part of the matching string with a range [0-5], hence we get a match from i0 to i5. You can also use the negation class ^ to filter the rest of the matches:

```
var strToMatch = 'i1,i2,i3,i4,i5,i6,i7,i8,i9';
var re = /i[^0-5]/gi;
var arrMatches = strToMatch.match(re);
console.log(arrMatches);
//["i6", "i7", "i8", "i9"]
```

Observe how we are negating only the range clause and not the entire expression.

Several character groups have shortcut notations. For example, the shortcut \d means the same thing as [0-9]:

Notation	Meaning
\d	Any digit character
\w	An alphanumeric character (word character)
\s	Any whitespace character (space, tab, newline, and similar)
\D	A character that is not a digit
\W	A non-alphanumeric character
\S	A non-whitespace character
.	Any character except for newline

These shortcuts are valuable in writing concise RegEx. Consider this example:

```
var strToMatch = '123-456-7890';
var re = /[0-9][0-9][0-9]-[0-9][0-9][0-9]/;
var arrMatches = strToMatch.match(re);
console.log(arrMatches);
//["123-456"]
```

This expression definitely looks a bit strange. We can replace `[0-9]` with `\d` and make this a bit more readable:

```
var strToMatch = '123-456-7890';
var re = /\d\d\d-\d\d\d/;
var arrMatches = strToMatch.match(re);
console.log(arrMatches);
//["123-456"]
```

However, you will soon see that there are even better ways to do something like this.

Repeated occurrences

So far, we saw how we can match fixed characters or numeric patterns. Most often, you want to handle certain repetitive natures of patterns also. For example, if I want to match 4 as, I can write `/aaaa/`, but what if I want to specify a pattern that can match any number of as?

Regular expressions provide you with a wide variety of repetition quantifiers. Repetition quantifiers let us specify how many times a particular pattern can occur. We can specify fixed values (characters should appear *n* times) and variable values (characters can appear at least *n* times till they appear *m* times). The following table lists the various repetition quantifiers:

- `?`: Either 0 or 1 occurrence (marks the occurrence as optional)
- `*`: 0 or more occurrences
- `+`: 1 or more occurrences
- `{n}`: Exactly n occurrences
- `{n,m}`: Occurrences between n and m
- `{n, }`: At least an n occurrence
- `{,n}`: 0 to n occurrences

In the following example, we create a pattern where the character u is optional (has 0 or 1 occurrence):

```
var str = /behaviou?r/;
console.log(str.test("behaviour"));
// true
console.log(str.test("behavior"));
// true
```

It helps to read the /behaviou?r/ expression as 0 or 1 occurrences of character u. The repetition quantifier succeeds the character that we want to repeat. Let's try out some more examples:

```
console.log(/'\d+'/.test("'123'")); // true
```

You should read and interpret the \d+ expression as ' is a literal character match, \d matches characters [0-9], the + quantifier will allow one or more occurrences, and ' is a literal character match.

You can also group character expressions using (). Observe the following example:

```
var heartyLaugh = /Ha+(Ha+)+/i;
console.log(heartyLaugh.test("HaHaHaHaHaHaHaaaaaaaaaaa"));
//true
```

Let's break the preceding expression into smaller chunks to understand what is going on in here:

- H: literal character match
- a+: 1 or more occurrences of character a
- (: start of the expression group
- H: literal character match
- a+: 1 or more occurrences of character a
-): end of expression group
- +: 1 or more occurrences of expression group (Ha+)

Now it is easier to see how the grouping is done. If we have to interpret the expression, it is sometimes helpful to read out the expression, as shown in the preceding example.

Often, you want to match a sequence of letters or numbers on their own and not just as a substring. This is a fairly common use case when you are matching words that are not just part of any other words. We can specify the word boundaries by using the \b pattern. The word boundary with \b matches the position where one side is a word character (letter, digit, or underscore) and the other side is not. Consider the following examples.

The following is a simple literal match. This match will also be successful if cat is part of a substring:

```
console.log(/cat/.test('a black cat')); //true
```

However, in the following example, we define a word boundary by indicating \b before the word cat — this means that we want to match only if cat is a word and not a substring. The boundary is established before cat, and hence a match is found on the text, a black cat:

```
console.log(/\bcat/.test('a black cat')); //true
```

When we use the same boundary with the word tomcat, we get a failed match because there is no word boundary before cat in the word tomcat:

```
console.log(/\bcat/.test('tomcat')); //false
```

There is a word boundary after the string cat in the word tomcat, hence the following is a successful match:

```
console.log(/cat\b/.test('tomcat')); //true
```

In the following example, we define the word boundary before and after the word cat to indicate that we want cat to be a standalone word with boundaries before and after:

```
console.log(/\bcat\b/.test('a black cat')); //true
```

Based on the same logic, the following match fails because there are no boundaries before and after cat in the word concatenate:

```
console.log(/\bcat\b/.test("concatenate")); //false
```

The `exec()` method is useful in getting information about the match found because it returns an object with information about the match. The object returned from `exec()` has an `index` property that tells us where the successful match begins in the string. This is useful in many ways:

```
var match = /\d+/.exec("There are 100 ways to do this");
console.log(match);
// ["100"]
console.log(match.index);
// 10
```

Alternatives – OR

Alternatives can be expressed using the | (pipe) character. For example, `/a|b/` matches either the a or b character, and `/(ab)+|(cd)+/` matches one or more occurrences of either ab or cd.

Beginning and end

Frequently, we may wish to ensure that a pattern matches at the beginning of a string or perhaps at the end of a string. The caret character, when used as the first character of the RegEx, anchors the match at the beginning of the string such that `/^test/` matches only if the test substring appears at the beginning of the string being matched. Similarly, the dollar sign ($) signifies that the pattern must appear at the end of the string: `/test$/`.

Using both ^ and $ indicates that the specified pattern must encompass the entire candidate string: `/^test$/`.

Backreferences

After an expression is evaluated, each group is stored for later use. These values are known as backreferences. Backreferences are created and numbered by the order in which opening parenthesis characters are encountered going from left to right. You can think of backreferences as the portions of a string that are successfully matched against terms in the regular expression.

The notation for a backreference is a backslash followed by the number of the capture to be referenced, beginning with 1, such as `\1`, `\2`, and so on.

An example could be /^([XYZ])a\1/, which matches a string that starts with any of the X, Y, or Z characters followed by an a and followed by whatever character matched the first capture. This is very different from /[XYZ]a[XYZ]/. The character following a can't be any of X, or Y, or Z, but must be whichever one of those that triggered the match for the first character. Backreferences are used with String's replace() method using the special character sequences, $1, $2, and so on. Suppose that you want to change the 1234 5678 string to 5678 1234. The following code accomplishes this:

```
var orig = "1234 5678";
var re = /(\d{4}) (\d{4})/;
var modifiedStr = orig.replace(re, "$2 $1");
console.log(modifiedStr); //outputs "5678 1234"
```

In this example, the regular expression has two groups each with four digits. In the second argument of the replace() method, $2 is equal to 5678 and $1 is equal to 1234, corresponding to the order in which they appear in the expression.

Greedy and lazy quantifiers

All the quantifiers that we discussed so far are greedy. A greedy quantifier starts looking at the entire string for a match. If there are no matches, it removes the last character in the string and reattempts the match. If a match is not found again, the last character is again removed and the process is repeated until a match is found or the string is left with no characters.

The \d+ pattern, for example, will match one or more digits. For example, if your string is 123, a greedy match would match 1, 12, and 123. Greedy pattern h.+l would match hell in a string hello—which is the longest possible string match. As \d+ is greedy, it will match as many digits as possible and hence the match would be 123.

In contrast to greedy quantifiers, a lazy quantifier matches as few of the quantified tokens as possible. You can add a question mark (?) to the regular expression to make it lazy. A lazy pattern h.?l would match hel in the string hello—which is the shortest possible string.

The \w*?X pattern will match zero or more words and then match an X. However, a question mark after * indicates that as few characters as possible should be matched. For an abcXXX string, the match can be abcX, abcXX, or abcXXX. Which one should be matched? As *? is lazy, as few characters as possible are matched and hence the match is abcX.

With this necessary information, let's try to solve some common problems using regular expressions.

Removing extra white space from the beginning and end of a string is a very common use case. As a String object did not have the `trim()` method until recently, several JavaScript libraries provide and use an implementation of string trimming for older browsers that don't have the `String.trim()` method. The most commonly used approach looks something like the following code:

```
function trim(str) {
    return (str || "").replace(/^\s+|\s+$/g, "");
}
console.log("--"+trim("   test   ")+"--");
//"--test--"
```

What if we want to replace repeated whitespaces with a single whitespace?

```
re=/\s+/g;
console.log('There are    a lot     of spaces'.replace(re,' '));
//"There are a lot of spaces"
```

In the preceding snippet, we are trying to match one or more space character sequences and replacing them with a single space.

As you can see, regular expressions can prove to be a Swiss army knife in your JavaScript arsenal. Careful study and practice will be extremely rewarding for you in the long run.

Arrays

An array is an ordered set of values. You can refer to the array elements with a name and index. These are the three ways to create arrays in JavaScript:

```
var arr = new Array(1,2,3);
var arr = Array(1,2,3);
var arr = [1,2,3];
```

When these values are specified, the array is initialized with them as the array's elements. An array's `length` property is equal to the number of arguments. The bracket syntax is called an array literal. It's a shorter and preferred way to initialize arrays.

You have to use the array literal syntax if you want to initialize an array with a single element and the element happens to be a number. If you pass a single number value to the `Array()` constructor or function, JavaScript considers this parameter as the length of the array, not as a single element:

```
var arr = [10];
var arr = Array(10); // Creates an array with no element, but with
  arr.length set to 10
// The above code is equivalent to
var arr = [];
arr.length = 10;
```

JavaScript does not have an explicit array data type. However, you can use the predefined `Array` object and its methods to work with arrays in your applications. The `Array` object has methods to manipulate arrays in various ways, such as joining, reversing, and sorting them. It has a property to determine the array length and other properties for use with regular expressions.

You can populate an array by assigning values to its elements:

```
var days = [];
days[0] = "Sunday";
days[1] = "Monday";
```

You can also populate an array when you create it:

```
var arr_generic = new Array("A String", myCustomValue, 3.14);
var fruits = ["Mango", "Apple", "Orange"]
```

In most languages, the elements of an array are all required to be of the same type. JavaScript allows an array to contain any type of values:

```
var arr = [
  'string', 42.0, true, false, null, undefined,
  ['sub', 'array'], {object: true}, NaN
];
```

You can refer to elements of an `Array` using the element's index number. For example, suppose you define the following array:

```
var days = ["Sunday", "Monday", "Tuesday"]
```

You then refer to the first element of the array as `colors[0]` and the second element of the array as `colors[1]`. The index of the elements starts with `0`.

JavaScript internally stores array elements as standard object properties, using the array index as the property name. The `length` property is different. The `length` property always returns the index of the last element plus one. As we discussed, JavaScript array indexes are 0-based: they start at 0, not 1. This means that the `length` property will be one more than the highest index stored in the array:

```
var colors = [];
colors[30] = ['Green'];
console.log(colors.length); // 31
```

You can also assign to the `length` property. Writing a value that is shorter than the number of stored items truncates the array; writing 0 empties it entirely:

```
var colors = ['Red', 'Blue', 'Yellow'];
console.log(colors.length); // 3
colors.length = 2;
console.log(colors); // ["Red","Blue"] - Yellow has been removed
colors.length = 0;
console.log(colors); // [] the colors array is empty
colors.length = 3;
console.log(colors); // [undefined, undefined, undefined]
```

If you query a non-existent array index, you get `undefined`.

A common operation is to iterate over the values of an array, processing each one in some way. The simplest way to do this is as follows:

```
var colors = ['red', 'green', 'blue'];
for (var i = 0; i < colors.length; i++) {
  console.log(colors[i]);
}
```

The `forEach()` method provides another way of iterating over an array:

```
var colors = ['red', 'green', 'blue'];
colors.forEach(function(color) {
  console.log(color);
});
```

The function passed to `forEach()` is executed once for every item in the array, with the array item passed as the argument to the function. Unassigned values are not iterated in a `forEach()` loop.

The `Array` object has a bunch of useful methods. These methods allow the manipulation of the data stored in the array.

The `concat()` method joins two arrays and returns a new array:

```
var myArray = new Array("33", "44", "55");
myArray = myArray.concat("3", "2", "1");
console.log(myArray);
// ["33", "44", "55", "3", "2", "1"]
```

The `join()` method joins all the elements of an array into a string. This can be useful while processing a list. The default delimiter is a comma (,):

```
var myArray = new Array('Red','Blue','Yellow');
var list = myArray.join(" ~ ");
console.log(list);
//"Red ~ Blue ~ Yellow"
```

The `pop()` method removes the last element from an array and returns that element. This is analogous to the `pop()` method of a stack:

```
var myArray = new Array("1", "2", "3");
var last = myArray.pop();
// myArray = ["1", "2"], last = "3"
```

The `push()` method adds one or more elements to the end of an array and returns the resulting length of the array:

```
var myArray = new Array("1", "2");
myArray.push("3");
// myArray = ["1", "2", "3"]
```

The `shift()` method removes the first element from an array and returns that element:

```
var myArray = new Array ("1", "2", "3");
var first = myArray.shift();
// myArray = ["2", "3"], first = "1"
```

The `unshift()` method adds one or more elements to the front of an array and returns the new length of the array:

```
var myArray = new Array ("1", "2", "3");
myArray.unshift("4", "5");
// myArray = ["4", "5", "1", "2", "3"]
```

The `reverse()` method reverses or transposes the elements of an array — the first array element becomes the last and the last becomes the first:

```
var myArray = new Array ("1", "2", "3");
myArray.reverse();
// transposes the array so that myArray = [ "3", "2", "1" ]
```

The `sort()` method sorts the elements of an array:

```
var myArray = new Array("A", "C", "B");
myArray.sort();
// sorts the array so that myArray = [ "A","B","C" ]
```

The `sort()` method can optionally take a callback function to define how the elements are compared. The function compares two values and returns one of three values. Let us study the following functions:

- `indexOf(searchElement[, fromIndex])`: This searches the array for `searchElement` and returns the index of the first match:

```
var a = ['a', 'b', 'a', 'b', 'a','c','a'];
console.log(a.indexOf('b')); // 1
// Now try again, starting from after the last match
console.log(a.indexOf('b', 2)); // 3
console.log(a.indexOf('1')); // -1, 'q' is not found
```

- `lastIndexOf(searchElement[, fromIndex])`: This works like `indexOf()`, but only searches backwards:

```
var a = ['a', 'b', 'c', 'd', 'a', 'b'];
console.log(a.lastIndexOf('b')); //  5
// Now try again, starting from before the last match
console.log(a.lastIndexOf('b', 4)); //  1
console.log(a.lastIndexOf('z')); //  -1
```

Now that we have covered JavaScript arrays in depth, let me introduce you to a fantastic library called **Underscore.js** (http://underscorejs.org/). Underscore.js provides a bunch of exceptionally useful functional programming helpers to make your code even more clear and functional.

We will assume that you are familiar with **Node.js**; in this case, install Underscore.js via npm:

```
npm install underscore
```

As we are installing Underscore as a Node module, we will test all the examples by typing them in a `.js` file and running the file on Node.js. You can install Underscore using **Bower** also.

Like jQuery's $ module, Underscore comes with a _ module defined. You will call all functions using this module reference.

Type the following code in a text file and name it `test_.js`:

```
var _ = require('underscore');
function print(n){
    console.log(n);
}
_.each([1, 2, 3], print);
//prints 1 2 3
```

This can be written as follows, without using `each()` function from underscore library:

```
var myArray = [1,2,3];
var arrayLength = myArray.length;
for (var i = 0; i < arrayLength; i++) {
    console.log(myArray[i]);
}
```

What you see here is a powerful functional construct that makes the code much more elegant and concise. You can clearly see that the traditional approach is verbose. Many languages such as Java suffer from this verbosity. They are slowly embracing functional paradigms. As JavaScript programmers, it is important for us to incorporate these ideas into our code as much as possible.

The `each()` function we saw in the preceding example iterates over a list of elements, yielding each to an iteratee function in turn. Each invocation of iteratee is called with three arguments (element, index, and list). In the preceding example, the `each()` function iterates over the array `[1,2,3]`, and for each element in the array, the `print` function is called with the array element as the parameter. This is a convenient alternative to the traditional looping mechanism to access all the elements in an array.

The `range()` function creates lists of integers. The start value, if omitted, defaults to `0` and step defaults to `1`. If you'd like a negative range, use a negative step:

```
var _ = require('underscore');
console.log(_.range(10));
// [0, 1, 2, 3, 4, 5, 6, 7, 8, 9 ]
console.log(_.range(1, 11));
//[ 1, 2, 3, 4, 5, 6, 7, 8, 9, 10 ]
console.log(_.range(0, 30, 5));
//[ 0, 5, 10, 15, 20, 25 ]
console.log(_.range(0, -10, -1));
//[ 0, -1, -2, -3, -4, -5, -6, -7, -8, -9 ]
console.log(_.range(0));
//[]
```

By default, `range()` populates the array with integers, but with a little trick, you can populate other data types also:

```
console.log(_.range(3).map(function () { return 'a' }) );
[ 'a', 'a', 'a' ]
```

This is a fast and convenient way to create and initialize an array with values. We frequently do this by traditional loops.

The `map()` function produces a new array of values by mapping each value in the list through a transformation function. Consider the following example:

```
var _ = require('underscore');
console.log(_.map([1, 2, 3], function(num){ return num * 3; }));
//[3,6,9]
```

The `reduce()` function reduces a list of values to a single value. The initial state is passed by the iteratee function and each successive step is returned by the iteratee. The following example shows the usage:

```
var _ = require('underscore');
var sum = _.reduce([1, 2, 3], function(memo, num){
   console.log(memo,num);return memo + num; }, 0);
console.log(sum);
```

In this example, the line, `console.log(memo,num);`, is just to make the idea clear. The output will be as follows:

```
0 1
1 2
3 3
6
```

The final output is a sum of *1+2+3=6*. As you can see, two values are passed to the iteratee function. On the first iteration, we call the iteratee function with two values `(0,1)` — the value of the `memo` is defaulted in the call to the `reduce()` function and `1` is the first element of the list. In the function, we sum `memo` and `num` and return the intermediate `sum`, which will be used by the `iterate()` function as a `memo` parameter — eventually, the `memo` will have the accumulated `sum`. This concept is important to understand how the intermediate states are used to calculate eventual results.

The `filter()` function iterates through the entire list and returns an array of all the elements that pass the condition. Take a look at the following example:

```
var _ = require('underscore');
var evens = _.filter([1, 2, 3, 4, 5, 6], function(num){
  return num % 2 == 0; });
console.log(evens);
```

The `filter()` function's iteratee function should return a truth value. The resulting `evens` array contains all the elements that satisfy the truth test.

The opposite of the `filter()` function is `reject()`. As the name suggests, it iterates through the list and ignores elements that satisfy the truth test:

```
var _ = require('underscore');
var odds = _.reject([1, 2, 3, 4, 5, 6], function(num){
  return num % 2 == 0; });
console.log(odds);
//[ 1, 3, 5 ]
```

We are using the same code as the previous example but using the `reject()` method instead of `filter()` — the result is exactly the opposite.

The `contains()` function is a useful little function that returns `true` if the value is present in the list; otherwise, returns `false`:

```
var _ = require('underscore');
console.log(_.contains([1, 2, 3], 3));
//true
```

One very useful function that I have grown fond of is `invoke()`. It calls a specific function on each element in the list. I can't tell you how many times I have used it since I stumbled upon it. Let us study the following example:

```
var _ = require('underscore');
console.log(_.invoke([[5, 1, 7], [3, 2, 1]], 'sort'));
//[ [ 1, 5, 7 ], [ 1, 2, 3 ] ]
```

In this example, the `sort()` method of the `Array` object is called for each element in the array. Note that this would fail:

```
var _ = require('underscore');
console.log(_.invoke(["new","old","cat"], 'sort'));
//[ undefined, undefined, undefined ]
```

This is because the `sort` method is not part of the String object. This, however, would work perfectly:

```
var _ = require('underscore');
console.log(_.invoke(["new","old","cat"], 'toUpperCase'));
//[ 'NEW', 'OLD', 'CAT' ]
```

This is because `toUpperCase()` is a String object method and all elements of the list are of the String type.

The `uniq()` function returns the array after removing all duplicates from the original one:

```
var _ = require('underscore');
var uniqArray = _.uniq([1,1,2,2,3]);
console.log(uniqArray);
//[1,2,3]
```

The `partition()` function splits the array into two; one whose elements satisfy the predicate and the other whose elements don't satisfy the predicate:

```
var _ = require('underscore');
function isOdd(n){
  return n%2==0;
}
console.log(_.partition([0, 1, 2, 3, 4, 5], isOdd));
//[ [ 0, 2, 4 ], [ 1, 3, 5 ] ]
```

The `compact()` function returns a copy of the array without all falsy values (false, null, 0, "", undefined, and NaN):

```
console.log(_.compact([0, 1, false, 2, '', 3]));
```

This snippet will remove all falsy values and return a new array with elements [1,2,3] — this is a helpful method to eliminate any value from a list that can cause runtime exceptions.

The `without()` function returns a copy of the array with all instances of the specific values removed:

```
var _ = require('underscore');
console.log(_.without([1,2,3,4,5,6,7,8,9,0,1,2,0,0,1,1],0,1,2));
//[ 3, 4, 5, 6, 7, 8, 9 ]
```

Maps

ECMAScript 6 introduces maps. A map is a simple key-value map and can iterate its elements in the order of their insertion. The following snippet shows some methods of the Map type and their usage:

```
var founders = new Map();
founders.set("facebook", "mark");
founders.set("google", "larry");
founders.size; // 2
founders.get("twitter"); // undefined
founders.has("yahoo"); // false

for (var [key, value] of founders) {
  console.log(key + " founded by " + value);
}
// "facebook founded by mark"
// "google founded by larry"
```

Sets

ECMAScript 6 introduces sets. Sets are collections of values and can be iterated in the order of the insertion of their elements. An important characteristic about sets is that a value can occur only once in a set.

The following snippet shows some basic operations on sets:

```
var mySet = new Set();
mySet.add(1);
mySet.add("Howdy");
mySet.add("foo");

mySet.has(1); // true
mySet.delete("foo");
mySet.size; // 2

for (let item of mySet) console.log(item);
// 1
// "Howdy"
```

We discussed briefly that JavaScript arrays are not really arrays in a traditional sense. In JavaScript, arrays are objects that have the following characteristics:

- The `length` property
- The functions that inherit from `Array.prototype` (we will discuss this in the next chapter)
- Special handling for keys that are numeric keys

When we write an array index as numbers, they get converted to strings — `arr[0]` internally becomes `arr["0"]`. Due to this, there are a few things that we need to be aware of when we use JavaScript arrays:

- Accessing array elements by an index is not a constant time operation as it is in, say, C. As arrays are actually key-value maps, the access will depend on the layout of the map and other factors (collisions and others).

- JavaScript arrays are sparse (most of the elements have the default value), which means that the array can have gaps in it. To understand this, look at the following snippet:

```
var testArr=new Array(3);
console.log(testArr);
```

You will see the output as `[undefined, undefined, undefined]` — `undefined` is the default value stored on the array element.

Consider the following example:

```
var testArr=[];
testArr[3] = 10;
testArr[10] = 3;
console.log(testArr);
// [undefined, undefined, undefined, 10, undefined, undefined,
   undefined, undefined, undefined, undefined, 3]
```

You can see that there are gaps in this array. Only two elements have elements and the rest are gaps with the default value. Knowing this helps you in a couple of things. Using the `for...in` loop to iterate an array can result in unexpected results. Consider the following example:

```
var a = [];
a[5] = 5;
for (var i=0; i<a.length; i++) {
  console.log(a[i]);
}
```

```
// Iterates over numeric indexes from 0 to 5
// [undefined,undefined,undefined,undefined,undefined,5]

for (var x in a) {
  console.log(x);
}
// Shows only the explicitly set index of "5", and ignores 0-4
```

A matter of style

Like the previous chapters, we will spend some time discussing the style considerations while creating arrays.

- Use the literal syntax for array creation:

```
// bad
const items = new Array();
// good
const items = [];
```

- Use `Array#push` instead of a direct assignment to add items to an array:

```
const stack = [];
// bad
stack[stack.length] = 'pushme';
// good
stack.push('pushme');
```

Summary

As JavaScript matures as a language, its tool chain also becomes more robust and effective. It is rare to see seasoned programmers staying away from libraries such as Underscore.js. As we see more advanced topics, we will continue to explore more such versatile libraries that can make your code compact, more readable, and performant. We looked at regular expressions—they are first-class objects in JavaScript. Once you start understanding `RegExp`, you will soon find yourself using more of them to make your code concise. In the next chapter, we will look at JavaScript Object notation and how JavaScript prototypal inheritance is a new way of looking at object-oriented programming.

Object-Oriented JavaScript

JavaScript's most fundamental data type is the Object data type. JavaScript objects can be seen as mutable key-value-based collections. In JavaScript, arrays, functions, and RegExp are objects while numbers, strings, and Booleans are object-like constructs that are immutable but have methods. In this chapter, you will learn the following topics:

- Understanding objects
- Instance properties versus prototype properties
- Inheritance
- Getters and setters

Understanding objects

Before we start looking at how JavaScript treats objects, we should spend some time on an object-oriented paradigm. Like most programming paradigms, **object-oriented programming** (OOP) also emerged from the need to manage complexity. The main idea is to divide the entire system into smaller pieces that are isolated from each other. If these small pieces can hide as many implementation details as possible, they become easy to use. A classic car analogy will help you understand this very important point about OOP.

When you drive a car, you operate on the interface—the steering, clutch, brake, and accelerator. Your view of using the car is limited by this interface, which makes it possible for us to drive the car. This interface is essentially hiding all the complex systems that really drive the car, such as the internal functioning of its engine, its electronic system, and so on. As a driver, you don't bother about these complexities. A similar idea is the primary driver of OOP. An object hides the complexities of how to implement a particular functionality and exposes a limited interface to the outside world. All other systems can use this interface without really bothering about the internal complexity that is hidden from view. Additionally, an object usually hides its internal state from other objects and prevents its direct modification. This is an important aspect of OOP.

In a large system where a lot of objects call other objects' interfaces, things can go really bad if you allow them to modify the internal state of such objects. OOP operates on the idea that the state of an object is inherently hidden from the outside world and it can be changed only via controlled interface operations.

OOP was an important idea and a definite step forward from the traditional structured programming. However, many feel that OOP is overdone. Most OOP systems define complex and unnecessary class and type hierarchies. Another big drawback was that in the pursuit of hiding the state, OOP considered the object state almost immaterial. Though hugely popular, OOP was clearly flawed in many areas. Still, OOP did have some very good ideas, especially hiding the complexity and exposing only the interface to the outside world. JavaScript picked up a few good ideas and built its object model around them. Luckily, this makes JavaScript objects very versatile. In their seminal work, *Design Patterns: Elements of Reusable Object-Oriented Software*, the *Gang of Four* gave two fundamental principles of a better object-oriented design:

- Program to an interface and not to an implementation
- Object composition over class inheritance

These two ideas are really against how classical OOP operates. The classical style of inheritance operates on inheritance that exposes parent classes to all child classes. Classical inheritance tightly couples children to its parents. There are mechanisms in classical inheritance to solve this problem to a certain extent. If you are using classical inheritance in a language such as Java, it is generally advisable to *program to an interface, not an implementation*. In Java, you can write a decoupled code using interfaces:

```
//programming to an interface 'List' and not implementation
  'ArrayList'
List theList = new ArrayList();
```

Instead of programming to an implementation, you can perform the following:

```
ArrayList theList = new ArrayList();
```

How does programming to an interface help? When you program to the `List` interface, you can call methods only available to the `List` interface and nothing specific to `ArrayList` can be called. Programming to an interface gives you the liberty to change your code and use any other specific child of the `List` interface. For example, I can change my implementation and use `LinkedList` instead of `ArrayList`. You can change your variable to use `LinkedList` instead:

```
List theList = new LinkedList();
```

The beauty of this approach is that if you are using the `List` at 100 places in your program, you don't have to worry about changing the implementation at all these places. As you were programming to the interface and not to the implementation, you were able to write a loosely coupled code. This is an important principle when you are using classical inheritance.

Classical inheritance also has a limitation where you can only enhance the child class within the limit of the parent classes. You can't fundamentally differ from what you have got from the ancestors. This inhibits reuse. Classical inheritance has several other problems as follows:

- Inheritance introduces tight coupling. Child classes have knowledge about their ancestors. This tightly couples a child class with its parent.

- When you subclass from a parent, you don't have a choice to select what you want to inherit and what you don't. *Joe Armstrong* (the inventor of **Erlang**) explains this situation very well — his now famous quote:

    "The problem with object-oriented languages is they've got all this implicit environment that they carry around with them. You wanted a banana but what you got was a gorilla holding the banana and the entire jungle."

Behavior of JavaScript objects

With this background, let's explore how JavaScript objects behave. In broad terms, an object contains properties, defined as a key-value pair. A property key (name) can be a string and the value can be any valid JavaScript value. You can create objects using object literals. The following snippet shows you how object literals are created:

```
var nothing = {};
var author = {
```

```
    "firstname": "Douglas",
    "lastname": "Crockford"
}
```

A property's name can be any string or an empty string. You can omit quotes around the property name if the name is a legal JavaScript name. So quotes are required around `first-name` but are optional around `firstname`. Commas are used to separate the pairs. You can nest objects as follows:

```
var author = {
  firstname : "Douglas",
  lastname : "Crockford",
  book : {
    title:"JavaScript- The Good Parts",
    pages:"172"
  }
};
```

Properties of an object can be accessed by using two notations: the array-like notation and dot notation. According to the array-like notation, you can retrieve the value from an object by wrapping a string expression in `[]`. If the expression is a valid JavaScript name, you can use the dot notation using `.` instead. Using `.` is a preferred method of retrieving values from an object:

```
console.log(author['firstname']); //Douglas
console.log(author.lastname);     //Crockford
console.log(author.book.title);   // JavaScript- The Good Parts
```

You will get an `undefined` error if you attempt to retrieve a non-existent value. The following would return `undefined`:

```
console.log(author.age);
```

A useful trick is to use the `||` operator to fill in default values in this case:

```
console.log(author.age || "No Age Found");
```

You can update values of an object by assigning a new value to the property:

```
author.book.pages = 190;
console.log(author.book.pages); //190
```

If you observe closely, you will realize that the object literal syntax that you see is very similar to the JSON format.

Methods are properties of an object that can hold function values as follows:

```
var meetingRoom = {};
meetingRoom.book = function(roomId){
  console.log("booked meeting room -"+roomId);
}
meetingRoom.book("VL");
```

Prototypes

Apart from the properties that we add to an object, there is one default property for almost all objects, called a **prototype**. When an object does not have a requested property, JavaScript goes to its prototype to look for it. The `Object.getPrototypeOf()` function returns the prototype of an object.

Many programmers consider prototypes closely related to objects' inheritance — they are indeed a way of defining object types — but fundamentally, they are closely associated with functions.

Prototypes are used as a way to define properties and functions that will be applied to instances of objects. The prototype's properties eventually become properties of the instantiated objects. Prototypes can be seen as blueprints for object creation. They can be seen as analogous to classes in object-oriented languages. Prototypes in JavaScript are used to write a classical style object-oriented code and mimic classical inheritance. Let's revisit our earlier example:

```
var author = {};
author.firstname = 'Douglas';
author.lastname = 'Crockford';
```

In the preceding code snippet, we are creating an empty object and assigning individual properties. You will soon realize that this is not a very standard way of building objects. If you know OOP already, you will immediately see that there is no encapsulation and the usual class structure. JavaScript provides a way around this. You can use the `new` operator to instantiate an object via constructors. However, there is no concept of a class in JavaScript, and it is important to note that the `new` operator is applied to the constructor function. To clearly understand this, let's look at the following example:

```
//A function that returns nothing and creates nothing
function Player() {}
```

```
//Add a function to the prototype property of the function
Player.prototype.usesBat = function() {
  return true;
}

//We call player() as a function and prove that nothing happens
var crazyBob = Player();
if(crazyBob === undefined){
  console.log("CrazyBob is not defined");
}

//Now we call player() as a constructor along with 'new'
//1. The instance is created
//2. method usesBat() is derived from the prototype of the function
var swingJay = new Player();
if(swingJay && swingJay.usesBat && swingJay.usesBat()){
  console.log("SwingJay exists and can use bat");
}
```

In the preceding example, we have a `player()` function that does nothing. We invoke it in two different ways. The first call of the function is as a normal function and second call is as a constructor—note the use of the `new()` operator in this call. Once the function is defined, we add a `usesBat()` method to it. When this function is called as a normal function, the object is not instantiated and we see `undefined` assigned to `crazyBob`. However, when we call this function with the `new` operator, we get a fully instantiated object, `swingJay`.

Instance properties versus prototype properties

Instance properties are the properties that are part of the object instance itself, as shown in the following example:

```
function Player() {
  this.isAvailable = function() {
    return "Instance method says - he is hired";
  };
}
Player.prototype.isAvailable = function() {
  return "Prototype method says - he is Not hired";
};
var crazyBob = new Player();
console.log(crazyBob.isAvailable());
```

When you run this example, you will see that **Instance method says - he is hired** is printed. The `isAvailable()` function defined in the `Player()` function is called an instance of `Player`. This means that apart from attaching properties via the prototype, you can use the this keyword to initialize properties in a constructor. When we have the same functions defined as an instance property and also as a prototype, the instance property takes precedence. The rules governing the precedence of the initialization are as follows:

- Properties are tied to the object instance from the prototype
- Properties are tied to the object instance in the constructor function

This example brings us to the use of the `this` keyword. It is easy to get confused by the `this` keyword because it behaves differently in JavaScript. In other OO languages such as Java, the `this` keyword refers to the current instance of the class. In JavaScript, the value of `this` is determined by the invocation context of a function and where it is called. Let's see how this behavior needs to be carefully understood:

- When `this` is used in a global context: When `this` is called in a global context, it is bound to the global context. For example, in the case of a browser, the global context is usually `window`. This is true for functions also. If you use `this` in a function that is defined in the global context, it is still bound to the global context because the function is part of the global context:

```
function globalAlias(){
  return this;
}
console.log(globalAlias()); //[object Window]
```

- When `this` is used in an object method: In this case, `this` is assigned or bound to the enclosing object. Note that the enclosing object is the immediate parent if you are nesting the objects:

```
var f = {
  name: "f",
  func: function () {
    return this;
  }
};
console.log(f.func());
//prints -
//[object Object] {
//  func: function () {
//    return this;
//  },
//  name: "f"
//}
```

- When there is no context: A function, when invoked without any object, does not get any context. By default, it is bound to the global context. When you use `this` in such a function, it is also bound to the global context.

- When `this` is used in a constructor function: As we saw earlier, when a function is called with a `new` keyword, it acts as a constructor. In the case of a constructor, `this` points to the object being constructed. In the following example, `f()` is used as a constructor (because it's invoked with a `new` keyword) and hence, `this` is pointing to the new object being created. So when we say `this.member = "f"`, the new member is added to the object being created, in this case, that object happens to be `o`:

```
var member = "global";
function f()
{
   this.member = "f";
}
var o= new f();
console.log(o.member); // f
```

We saw that instance properties take precedence when the same property is defined both as an instance property and prototype property. It is easy to visualize that when a new object is created, the properties of the constructor's prototype are copied over. However, this is not a correct assumption. What actually happens is that the prototype is attached to the object and referred when any property of this object is referred. Essentially, when a property is referenced on an object, either of the following occur:

- The object is checked for the existence of the property. If it's found, the property is returned.

- The associated prototype is checked. If the property is found, it is returned; otherwise, an `undefined` error is returned.

This is an important understanding because, in JavaScript, the following code actually works perfectly:

```
function Player() {
   isAvailable=false;
}
var crazyBob = new Player();
Player.prototype.isAvailable = function() {
   return isAvailable;
};
console.log(crazyBob.isAvailable()); //false
```

This code is a slight variation of the earlier example. We are creating the object first and then attaching the function to its prototype. When you eventually call the `isAvailable()` method on the object, JavaScript goes to its prototype to search for it if it's not found in the particular object (`crazyBob`, in this case). Think of this as *hot code loading*—when used properly, this ability can give you incredible power to extend the basic object framework even after the object is created.

If you are familiar with OOP already, you must be wondering whether we can control the visibility and access of the members of an object. As we discussed earlier, JavaScript does not have classes. In programming languages such as Java, you have access modifiers such as `private` and `public` that let you control the visibility of the class members. In JavaScript, we can achieve something similar using the function scope as follows:

- You can declare private variables using the `var` keyword in a function. They can be accessed by private functions or privileged methods.
- Private functions may be declared in an object's constructor and can be called by privileged methods.
- Privileged methods can be declared with `this.method=function() {}`.
- Public methods are declared with `Class.prototype.method=function() {}`.
- Public properties can be declared with `this.property` and accessed from outside the object.

The following example shows several ways of doing this:

```
function Player(name,sport,age,country){

    this.constructor.noOfPlayers++;

    // Private Properties and Functions
    // Can only be viewed, edited or invoked by privileged members
    var retirementAge = 40;
    var available=true;
    var playerAge = age?age:18;
    function isAvailable(){ return available &&
(playerAge<retirementAge); }
    var playerName=name ? name :"Unknown";
    var playerSport = sport ? sport : "Unknown";
```

```
// Privileged Methods
// Can be invoked from outside and can access private members
// Can be replaced with public counterparts
this.book=function(){
  if (!isAvailable()){
    this.available=false;
  } else {
    console.log("Player is unavailable");
  }
};
this.getSport=function(){ return playerSport; };
// Public properties, modifiable from anywhere
this.batPreference="Lefty";
this.hasCelebGirlfriend=false;
this.endorses="Super Brand";
}


// Public methods - can be read or written by anyone
// Can only access public and prototype properties
Player.prototype.switchHands = function(){ this.
batPreference="righty"; };
Player.prototype.dateCeleb = function(){ this.hasCelebGirlfriend=true;
} ;
Player.prototype.fixEyes = function(){ this.wearGlasses=false; };


// Prototype Properties - can be read or written by anyone (or
overridden)
Player.prototype.wearsGlasses=true;


// Static Properties - anyone can read or write
Player.noOfPlayers = 0;



(function PlayerTest(){
  //New instance of the Player object created.
  var cricketer=new Player("Vivian","Cricket",23,"England");
  var golfer =new Player("Pete","Golf",32,"USA");
  console.log("So far there are " + Player.noOfPlayers + " in the
guild");
```

```
  //Both these functions share the common 'Player.prototype.
wearsGlasses' variable
  cricketer.fixEyes();
  golfer.fixEyes();


  cricketer.endorses="Other Brand";//public variable can be updated

  //Both Player's public method is now changed via their prototype
  Player.prototype.fixEyes=function(){
    this.wearGlasses=true;
  };
  //Only Cricketer's function is changed
  cricketer.switchHands=function(){
    this.batPreference="undecided";
  };

})();
```

Let's understand a few important concepts from this example:

- The retirementAge variable is a private variable that has no privileged method to get or set its value.

- The country variable is a private variable created as a constructor argument. Constructor arguments are available as private variables to the object.

- When we called cricketer.switchHands(), it was only applied to the cricketer and not to both the players, although it's a prototype function of the Player itself.

- Private functions and privileged methods are instantiated with each new object created. In our example, new copies of isAvailable() and book() would be created for each new player instance that we create. On the other hand, only one copy of public methods is created and shared between all instances. This can mean a bit of performance gain. If you don't *really* need to make something private, think about keeping it public.

Inheritance

Inheritance is an important concept of OOP. It is common to have a bunch of objects implementing the same methods. It is also common to have an almost similar object definition with differences in a few methods. Inheritance is very useful in promoting code reuse. We can look at the following classic example of inheritance relation:

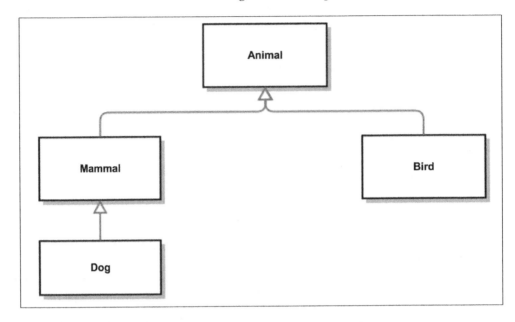

Here, you can see that from the generic **Animal** class, we derive more specific classes such as **Mammal** and **Bird** based on specific characteristics. Both the Mammal and Bird classes do have the same template of an Animal; however, they also define behaviors and attributes specific to them. Eventually, we derive a very specific mammal, **Dog**. A Dog has common attributes and behaviors from an Animal class and Mammal class, while it adds specific attributes and behaviors of a Dog. This can go on to add complex inheritance relationships.

Traditionally, inheritance is used to establish or describe an **IS-A** relationship. For example, a dog IS-A mammal. This is what we know as **classical inheritance**. You would have seen such relationships in object-oriented languages such as C++ and Java. JavaScript has a completely different mechanism to handle inheritance. JavaScript is classless language and uses prototypes for inheritance. Prototypal inheritance is very different in nature and needs thorough understanding. Classical and prototypal inheritance are very different in nature and need careful study.

In classical inheritance, instances inherit from a class blueprint and create subclass relationships. You can't invoke instance methods on a class definition itself. You need to create an instance and then invoke methods on this instance. In prototypal inheritance, on the other hand, instances inherit from other instances.

As far as inheritance is concerned, JavaScript uses only objects. As we discussed earlier, each object has a link to another object called its prototype. This prototype object, in turn, has a prototype of its own, and so on until an object is reached with `null` as its prototype; `null`, by definition, has no prototype, and acts as the final link in this prototype chain.

To understand prototype chains better, let's consider the following example:

```javascript
function Person() {}
Person.prototype.cry = function() {
  console.log("Crying");
}
function Child() {}
Child.prototype = {cry: Person.prototype.cry};
var aChild = new Child();
console.log(aChild instanceof Child);   //true
console.log(aChild instanceof Person); //false
console.log(aChild instanceof Object); //true
```

Here, we define a `Person` and then `Child`—a child IS-A person. We also copy the `cry` property of a `Person` to the `cry` property of `Child`. When we try to see this relationship using `instanceof`, we soon realize that just by copying a behavior, we could not really make `Child` an instance of `Person`; aChild `instanceof` Person fails. This is just copying or masquerading, not inheritance. Even if we copy all the properties of `Person` to `Child`, we won't be inheriting from `Person`. This is usually a bad idea and is shown here only for illustrative purposes. We want to derive a prototype chain—an IS-A relationship, a real inheritance where we can say that child IS-A person. We want to create a chain: a child IS-A person IS-A mammal IS-A animal IS-A object. In JavaScript, this is done using an instance of an object as a prototype as follows:

```javascript
SubClass.prototype = new SuperClass();
Child.prototype = new Person();
```

Let's modify the earlier example:

```javascript
function Person() {}
Person.prototype.cry = function() {
  console.log("Crying");
}
```

```
function Child() {}
Child.prototype = new Person();
var aChild = new Child();
console.log(aChild instanceof Child);  //true
console.log(aChild instanceof Person); //true
console.log(aChild instanceof Object); //true
```

The changed line uses an instance of Person as the prototype of Child. This is an important distinction from the earlier method. Here we are declaring that child IS-A person.

We discussed about how JavaScript looks for a property up the prototype chain till it reaches Object.prototype. Let's discuss the concept of prototype chains in detail and try to design the following employee hierarchy:

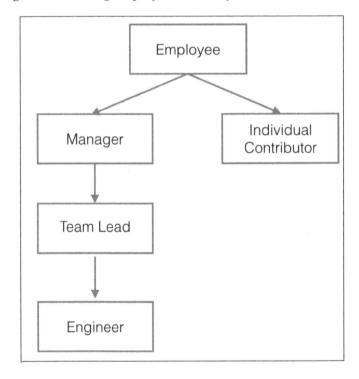

This is a typical pattern of inheritance. A manager IS-A(n) employee. **Manager** has common properties inherited from an **Employee**. It can have an array of reportees. An **Individual Contributor** is also based on an employee but he does not have any reportees. A **Team Lead** is derived from a Manager with a few functions that are different from a Manager. What we are doing essentially is that each child is deriving properties from its parent (Manager being the parent and Team Lead being the child).

Let's see how we can create this hierarchy in JavaScript. Let's define our `Employee` type:

```
function Employee() {
    this.name = '';
    this.dept = 'None';
    this.salary = 0.00;
}
```

There is nothing special about these definitions. The `Employee` object contains three properties—name, salary, and department. Next, we define `Manager`. This definition shows you how to specify the next object in the inheritance chain:

```
function Manager() {
    Employee.call(this);
    this.reports = [];
}
Manager.prototype = Object.create(Employee.prototype);
```

In JavaScript, you can add a prototypical instance as the value of the prototype property of the constructor function. You can do so at any time after you define the constructor. In this example, there are two ideas that we have not explored earlier. First, we are calling `Employee.call(this)`. If you come from a Java background, this is analogous to the `super()` method call in the constructor. The `call()` method calls a function with a specific object as its context (in this case, it is the given the `this` value), in other words, call allows to specify which object will be referenced by the `this` keyword when the function will be executed. Like `super()` in Java, calling `parentObject.call(this)` is necessary to correctly initialize the object being created.

The other thing we see is `Object.create()` instead of calling new. `Object.create()` creates an object with a specified prototype. When we do `new Parent()`, the constructor logic of the parent is called. In most cases, what we want is for `Child.prototype` to be an object that is linked via its prototype to `Parent.prototype`. If the parent constructor contains additional logic specific to the parent, we don't want to run this while creating the child object. This can cause very difficult-to-find bugs. `Object.create()` creates the same prototypal link between the child and parent as the new operator without calling the parent constructor.

To have a side effect-free and accurate inheritance mechanism, we have to make sure that we perform the following:

- Setting the prototype to an instance of the parent initializes the prototype chain (inheritance); this is done only once (as the prototype object is shared)
- Calling the parent's constructor initializes the object itself; this is done with every instantiation (you can pass different parameters each time you construct it)

With this understanding in place, let's define the rest of the objects:

```
function IndividualContributor() {
  Employee.call(this);
  this.active_projects = [];
}
IndividualContributor.prototype = Object.create(Employee.prototype);

function TeamLead() {
  Manager.call(this);
  this.dept = "Software";
  this.salary = 100000;
}
TeamLead.prototype = Object.create(Manager.prototype);

function Engineer() {
  TeamLead.call(this);
  this.dept = "JavaScript";
  this.desktop_id = "8822" ;
  this.salary = 80000;
}
Engineer.prototype = Object.create(TeamLead.prototype);
```

Based on this hierarchy, we can instantiate these objects:

```
var genericEmployee = new Employee();
console.log(genericEmployee);
```

You can see the following output for the preceding code snippet:

```
[object Object] {
  dept: "None",
  name: "",
  salary: 0
}
```

A generic `Employee` has a department assigned to `None` (as specified in the default value) and the rest of the properties are also assigned as the default ones.

Next, we instantiate a manager; we can provide specific values as follows:

```
var karen = new Manager();
karen.name = "Karen";
karen.reports = [1,2,3];
console.log(karen);
```

You will see the following output:

```
[object Object] {
  dept: "None",
  name: "Karen",
  reports: [1, 2, 3],
  salary: 0
}
```

For `TeamLead`, the `reports` property is derived from the base class (Manager in this case):

```
var jason = new TeamLead();
jason.name = "Json";
console.log(jason);
```

You will see the following output:

```
[object Object] {
  dept: "Software",
  name: "Json",
  reports: [],
  salary: 100000
}
```

When JavaScript processes the new operator, it creates a new object and passes this object as the value of `this` to the parent—the `TeamLead` constructor. The constructor function sets the value of the `projects` property and implicitly sets the value of the internal `__proto__` property to the value of `TeamLead.prototype`. The `__proto__` property determines the prototype chain used to return property values. This process does not set values for properties inherited from the prototype chain in the `jason` object. When the value of a property is read, JavaScript first checks to see whether the value exists in that object. If the value does exist, this value is returned. If the value is not there, JavaScript checks the prototype chain using the `__proto__` property. Having said this, what happens when you do the following:

```
Employee.prototype.name = "Undefined";
```

It does not propagate to all the instances of `Employee`. This is because when you create an instance of the `Employee` object, this instance gets a local value for the name. When you set the `TeamLead` prototype by creating a new `Employee` object, `TeamLead.prototype` has a local value for the `name` property. Therefore, when JavaScript looks up the `name` property of the `jason` object, which is an instance of `TeamLead`), it finds the local value for this property in `TeamLead.prototype`. It does not try to do further lookups up the chain to `Employee.prototype`.

If you want the value of a property changed at runtime and have the new value be inherited by all the descendants of the object, you cannot define the property in the object's constructor function. To achieve this, you need to add it to the constructor's prototype. For example, let's revisit the earlier example but with a slight change:

```
function Employee() {
   this.dept = 'None';
   this.salary = 0.00;
}
Employee.prototype.name = '';
function Manager() {
   this.reports = [];
}
Manager.prototype = new Employee();
var sandy = new Manager();
var karen = new Manager();

Employee.prototype.name = "Junk";

console.log(sandy.name);
console.log(karen.name);
```

You will see that the name property of both sandy and karen has changed to Junk. This is because the name property is declared outside the constructor function. So, when you change the value of name in the Employee's prototype, it propagates to all the descendants. In this example, we are modifying Employee's prototype after the sandy and karen objects are created. If you changed the prototype before the sandy and karen objects were created, the value would still have changed to Junk.

All native JavaScript objects—Object, Array, String, Number, RegExp, and Function—have prototype properties that can be extended. This means that we can extend the functionality of the language itself. For example, the following snippet extends the String object to add a reverse() method to reverse a string. This method does not exist in the native String object but by manipulating String's prototype, we add this method to String:

```
String.prototype.reverse = function() {
    return Array.prototype.reverse.apply(this.split('')).join('');
};
var str = 'JavaScript';
console.log(str.reverse()); //"tpircSavaJ"
```

Though this is a very powerful technique, care should be taken not to overuse it. Refer to http://perfectionkills.com/extending-native-builtins/ to understand the pitfalls of extending native built-ins and what care should be taken if you intend to do so.

Getters and setters

Getters are convenient methods to get the value of specific properties; as the name suggests, **setters** are methods that set the value of a property. Often, you may want to derive a value based on some other values. Traditionally, getters and setters used to be functions such as the following:

```
var person = {
    firstname: "Albert",
    lastname: "Einstein",
    setLastName: function(_lastname){
        this.lastname= _lastname;
    },
    setFirstName: function (_firstname){
        this.firstname= _firstname;
    },
    getFullName: function (){
        return this.firstname + ' '+ this.lastname;
    }
};
person.setLastName('Newton');
person.setFirstName('Issac');
console.log(person.getFullName());
```

As you can see, setLastName(), setFirstName(), and getFullName() are functions used to do *get* and *set* of properties. Fullname is a derived property by concatenating the firstname and lastname properties. This is a very common use case and ECMAScript 5 now provides you with a default syntax for getters and setters.

The following example shows you how getters and setters are created using the object literal syntax in ECMAScript 5:

```
var person = {
  firstname: "Albert",
  lastname: "Einstein",
  get fullname() {
    return this.firstname +" "+this.lastname;
  },
  set fullname(_name){
    var words = _name.toString().split(' ');
    this.firstname = words[0];
    this.lastname = words[1];
  }
};
person.fullname = "Issac Newton";
console.log(person.firstname); //"Issac"
console.log(person.lastname);  //"Newton"
console.log(person.fullname);  //"Issac Newton"
```

Another way of declaring getters and setters is using the `Object.defineProperty()` method:

```
var person = {
  firstname: "Albert",
  lastname: "Einstein",
};
Object.defineProperty(person, 'fullname', {
  get: function() {
    return this.firstname + ' ' + this.lastname;
  },
  set: function(name) {
    var words = name.split(' ');
    this.firstname = words[0];
    this.lastname = words[1];
  }
});
person.fullname = "Issac Newton";
console.log(person.firstname); //"Issac"
console.log(person.lastname);  //"Newton"
console.log(person.fullname);  //"Issac Newton"
```

In this method, you can call `Object.defineProperty()` even after the object is created.

Now that you have tasted the object-oriented flavor of JavaScript, we will go through a bunch of very useful utility methods provided by **Underscore.js**. We discussed the installation and basic usage of Underscore.js in the previous chapter. These methods will make common operations on objects very easy:

- `keys()`: This method retrieves the names of an object's own enumerable properties. Note that this function does not traverse up the prototype chain:

```
var _ = require('underscore');
var testobj = {
  name: 'Albert',
  age : 90,
  profession: 'Physicist'
};
console.log(_.keys(testobj));
//[ 'name', 'age', 'profession' ]
```

- `allKeys()`: This method retrieves the names of an object's own and inherited properties:

```
var _ = require('underscore');
function Scientist() {
  this.name = 'Albert';
}
Scientist.prototype.married = true;
aScientist = new Scientist();
console.log(_.keys(aScientist)); //[ 'name' ]
console.log(_.allKeys(aScientist));//[ 'name', 'married' ]
```

- `values()`: This method retrieves the values of an object's own properties:

```
var _ = require('underscore');
function Scientist() {
  this.name = 'Albert';
}
Scientist.prototype.married = true;
aScientist = new Scientist();
console.log(_.values(aScientist)); //[ 'Albert' ]
```

- `mapObject()`: This method transforms the value of each property in the object:

```
var _ = require('underscore');
function Scientist() {
  this.name = 'Albert';
  this.age = 90;
}
```

```
aScientist = new Scientist();
var lst = _.mapObject(aScientist, function(val,key){
  if(key==="age"){
    return val + 10;
  } else {
    return val;
  }
});
console.log(lst); //{ name: 'Albert', age: 100 }
```

- `functions()`: This returns a sorted list of the names of every method in an object—the name of every function property of the object.

- `pick()`: This function returns a copy of the object, filtered to just the values of the keys provided:

```
var _ = require('underscore');
var testobj = {
  name: 'Albert',
  age : 90,
  profession: 'Physicist'
};
console.log(_.pick(testobj, 'name','age')); //{ name: 'Albert',
age: 90 }
console.log(_.pick(testobj, function(val,key,object){
  return _.isNumber(val);
})); //{ age: 90 }
```

- `omit()`: This function is an invert of `pick()`—it returns a copy of the object, filtered to omit the values for the specified keys.

Summary

JavaScript applications can improve in clarity and quality by allowing for the greater degree of control and structure that object-orientation can bring to the code. JavaScript object-orientation is based on the function prototypes and prototypal inheritance. These two ideas can provide an incredible amount of wealth to developers.

In this chapter, we saw basic object creation and manipulation. We looked at how constructor functions are used to create objects. We dived into prototype chains and how inheritance operates on the idea of prototype chains. These foundations will be used to build your knowledge of JavaScript patterns that we will explore in the next chapter.

5
JavaScript Patterns

So far, we have looked at several fundamental building blocks necessary to write code in JavaScript. Once you start building larger systems using these fundamental constructs, you soon realize that there can be a standard way of doing a few things. While developing a large system, you will encounter repetitive problems; a pattern intends to provide a standardized solution to such known and identified problems. A pattern can be seen as a best practice, useful abstraction, or template to solve common problems. Writing maintainable code is difficult. The key to write modular, correct, and maintainable code is the ability to understand the repeating themes and use common templates to write optimized solutions to these. The most important text on design patterns was a book published in 1995 called *Design Patterns: Elements Of Reusable Object-Oriented Software* written by *Erich Gamma, Richard Helm, Ralph Johnson, and John Vlissides* — a group that became known as the **Gang of Four** (**GOF** for short). This seminal work gave a formal definition to various patterns and explained implementation details of most of the popular patterns that we use today. It is important to understand why patterns are important:

- Patterns offer proven solutions to common problems: Patterns provide templates that are optimized to solve a particular problem. These patterns are backed by solid engineering experience and tested for validity.

- Patterns are designed to be reused: They are generic enough to fit variations of a problem.

- Patterns define vocabulary: Patterns are well-defined structures and hence provide a generic vocabulary to the solution. This can be very expressive when communicating across a larger group.

Design patterns

In this chapter, we will take a look at some of the design patterns that make sense for JavaScript. However, coding patterns are very specific for JavaScript and are of great interest to us. While we spend a lot of time and effort trying to understand and master design patterns, it is important to understand anti-patterns and how to avoid pitfalls. In the usual software development cycle, there are several places where bad code is introduced, mainly around the time where the code is nearing a release or when the code is handed over to a different team for maintenance. If such bad design constructs are documented as anti-patterns, they can provide guidance to developers in knowing what pitfalls to avoid and how not to subscribe to bad design patterns. Most languages have their set of anti-patterns. Based on the kind of problems that they solve, design patterns were categorized into a few broad categories by the GOF:

- **Creational design patterns**: These patterns deal with various mechanisms of object creation. While most languages provide basic object creation methods, these patterns look at optimized or more controlled mechanisms of object creation.

- **Structural design patterns**: These patterns are all about the composition of objects and relationships among them. The idea is to have minimal impact on overall object relationships when something in the system changes.

- **Behavioral design patterns**: These patterns focus on the interdependency and communication between objects.

The following table is a useful ready reckoner to identify categories of patterns:

- Creational patterns:
    - Factory method
    - Abstract factory
    - Builder
    - Prototype
    - Singleton

- Structural patterns:
    - Adapter
    - Bridge
    - Composite
    - Decorator
    - Façade

- ° Flyweight
- ° Proxy

- Behavioral patterns

  - ° Interpreter
  - ° Template method
  - ° Chain of responsibility
  - ° Command
  - ° Iterator
  - ° Mediator
  - ° Memento
  - ° Observer
  - ° State
  - ° Strategy
  - ° Visitor

Some patterns that we will discuss in this chapter may not be part of this list as they are more specific to JavaScript or a variation of these classical patterns. Similarly, we will not discuss patterns that do not fit into JavaScript or are not in popular use.

The namespace pattern

Excessive use of the global scope is almost a taboo in JavaScript. When you build larger programs, it is sometimes difficult to control how much the global scope is polluted. Namespace can reduce the number of globals created by the program and also helps in avoiding naming collisions or excessive name prefixing. The idea of using namespaces is creating a global object for your application or library and adding all these objects and functions to that object rather than polluting the global scope with objects. JavaScript doesn't have an explicit syntax for namespaces, but namespaces can be easily created. Let's consider the following example:

```
function Car() {}
function BMW() {}
var engines = 1;
var features = {
  seats: 6,
  airbags:6
};
```

We are creating all this in the global scope. This is an anti-pattern, and this is never a good idea. We can, however, refactor this code and create a single global object and make all the functions and objects part of this global object as follows:

```
// Single global object
var CARFACTORY = CARFACTORY || {};
CARFACTORY.Car = function () {};
CARFACTORY.BMW = function () {};
CARFACTORY.engines = 1;
CARFACTORY.features = {
  seats: 6,
  airbags:6
};
```

By convention, the global namespace object name is generally written in all caps. This pattern adds namespace to the application and prevents naming collisions in your code and between your code and external library that you use. Many projects use a distinct name after their company or project to create a unique name for their namespace.

Though this seems like an ideal way to restrict your globals and add a namespace to your code, it is a bit verbose; you need to prefix every variable and function with the namespace. You need to type more and the code becomes unnecessarily verbose. Additionally, a single global instance would mean that any part of the code can modify the global instance and the rest of the functionality gets the updated state—this can cause very nasty side-effects. A curious thing to observe in the earlier example is this line— `var CARFACTORY = CARFACTORY || {};`. When you are working on a large code base, you can't assume that you are creating this namespace (or assigning a property to it) for the first time. It is possible that the namespace may pre-exist. To make sure that you create the namespace only if it is not already created, it is safe to always rely on the quick defaulting via a short-circuit || operator.

The module pattern

As you build large applications, you will soon realize that it becomes increasingly difficult to keep the code base organized and modular. The module patterns help in keeping the code cleanly separated and organized.

Module separates bigger programs into smaller pieces and gives them a namespace. This is very important because once you separate code into modules, these modules can be reused in several places. Carefully designing interfaces for the modules will make your code very easy to reuse and extend.

JavaScript offers flexible functions and objects that make it easy to create robust module systems. Function scopes help create namespaces that are internal for the module, and objects can be used to store sets of exported values.

Before we start exploring the pattern itself, let's quickly brush up on a few concepts that we discussed earlier.

We discussed object literals in detail. Object literals allow you to create name-value pairs as follows:

```
var basicServerConfig = {
  environment: "production",
  startupParams: {
    cacheTimeout: 30,
    locale: "en_US"
  },
  init: function () {
    console.log( "Initializing the server" );
  },
  updateStartup: function( params ) {
      this.startupParams = params;
      console.log( this.startupParams.cacheTimeout );
      console.log( this.startupParams.locale );
  }
};
basicServerConfig.init(); //"Initializing the server"
basicServerConfig.updateStartup({cacheTimeout:60,
  locale:"en_UK"}); //60, en_UK
```

In this example, we are creating an object literal and defining key-value pairs to create properties and functions.

In JavaScript, the module pattern is used very heavily. Modules help in mimicking the concept of classes. Modules allow us to include both public/private methods and variables of an object, but most importantly, modules restrict these parts from the global scope. As the variables and functions are contained in the module scope, we automatically prevent naming conflict with other scripts using the same names.

Another beautiful aspect of the module pattern is that we expose only a public API. Everything else related to the internal implementation is held private within the module's closure.

Unlike other OO languages, JavaScript has no explicit access modifiers and, hence, there is no concept of *privacy*. You can't have public or private variables. As we discussed earlier, in JavaScript, the function scope can be used to enforce this concept. The module pattern uses closures to restrict variable and function access only within the module; however, variables and functions are defined in the object being returned, which is available to the public.

Let's consider the earlier example and turn this into a module. We are essentially using an IIFE and returning the interface of the module, namely, the `init` and `updateStartup` functions:

```
var basicServerConfig = (function () {
  var environment= "production";
  startupParams= {
    cacheTimeout: 30,
    locale: "en_US"
  };
  return {
    init: function () {
      console.log( "Initializing the server" );
    },
    updateStartup: function( params ) {
      this.startupParams = params;
      console.log( this.startupParams.cacheTimeout );
      console.log( this.startupParams.locale );
    }
  };
})();
basicServerConfig.init(); //"Initializing the server"
basicServerConfig.updateStartup({cacheTimeout:60,
  locale:"en_UK"}); //60, en_UK
```

In this example, `basicServerConfig` is created as a module in the global context. To make sure that we are not polluting the global context with modules, it is important to create namespaces for the modules. Moreover, as modules are inherently reused, it is important to make sure that we avoid naming conflicts using namespaces. For the `basicServerConfig` module, the following snippet shows you the way to create a namespace:

```
// Single global object
var SERVER = SERVER||{};
SERVER.basicServerConfig = (function () {
  Var environment= "production";
  startupParams= {
```

```
      cacheTimeout: 30,
      locale: "en_US"
    };
    return {
      init: function () {
        console.log( "Initializing the server" );
      },
      updateStartup: function( params ) {
        this.startupParams = params;
        console.log( this.startupParams.cacheTimeout );
        console.log( this.startupParams.locale );
      }
    };
  })();
  SERVER.basicServerConfig.init(); //"Initializing the server"
  SERVER.basicServerConfig.updateStartup({cacheTimeout:60,
    locale:"en_UK"}); //60, en_UK
```

Using namespace with modules is generally a good idea; however, it is not required that a module must have a namespace associated.

A variation of the module pattern tries to overcome a few problems of the original module pattern. This improved variation of the module pattern is also known as the **revealing module pattern (RMP)**. RMP was first popularized by *Christian Heilmann*. He disliked that it was necessary to use the module name while calling a public function from another function or accessing a public variable. Another small problem is that you have to use an object literal notation while returning the public interface. Consider the following example:

```
var modulePattern = function(){
  var privateOne = 1;
  function privateFn(){
    console.log('privateFn called');
  }
  return {
    publicTwo: 2,
    publicFn:function(){
      modulePattern.publicFnTwo();
    },
    publicFnTwo:function(){
      privateFn();
    }
  }
}();
modulePattern.publicFn(); "privateFn called"
```

You can see that we need to call `publicFnTwo()` via `modulePattern` in `publicFn()`. Additionally, the public interface is returned in an object literal. The improvement on the classic module pattern is what is known as the RMP. The primary idea behind this pattern is to define all of the members in the private scope and return an anonymous object with pointers to the private functionality that needs to be revealed as public.

Let's see how we can convert our previous example to an RMP. This example is heavily inspired from Christian's blog:

```
var revealingExample = function(){
  var privateOne = 1;
  function privateFn(){
    console.log('privateFn called');
  }
  var publicTwo = 2;
  function publicFn(){
    publicFnTwo();
  }
  function publicFnTwo(){
    privateFn();
  }
  function getCurrentState(){
    return 2;
  }
  // reveal private variables by assigning public pointers
  return {
    setup:publicFn,
    count:publicTwo,
    increaseCount:publicFnTwo,
    current:getCurrentState()
  };
}();
console.log(revealingExample.current); // 2
revealingExample.setup(); //privateFn called
```

An important distinction here is that you define functions and variables in the private scope and return an anonymous object with pointers to the private variables and functions that you want to reveal as public. This is a much cleaner variation and should be preferred over the classic module pattern.

In production code, however, you would want to use more a standardized approach to create modules. Currently, there are two main approaches to create modules. The first is known as **CommonJS modules**. CommonJS modules are usually more suited for server-side JavaScript environments such as **Node.js**. A CommonJS module contains a `require()` function that receives the name of the module and returns the module's interface. The format was proposed by the volunteer group of CommonJS; their aim was to design, prototype, and standardize JavaScript APIs. CommonJS modules consist of two parts. Firstly, list of variables and functions the module needs to expose; when you assign a variable or function to the `module.exports` variable, it is exposed from the module. Secondly, a `require` function that modules can use to import the exports of other modules:

```
//Add a dependency module
var crypto = require('crypto');
function randomString(length, chars) {
  var randomBytes = crypto.randomBytes(length);
  . . .
  . . .
}
//Export this module to be available for other modules
module.exports=randomString;
```

CommonJS modules are supported by Node.js on the server and **curl.js** in the browser.

The other flavor of JavaScript modules is called **Asynchronous Module Definition (AMD)**. They are browser-first modules and opt for asynchronous behavior. AMD uses a `define` function to define the modules. This function takes an array of module names and a function. Once the modules are loaded, the `define` function executes the function with their interface as an argument. The AMD proposal is aimed at the asynchronous loading of both the module and dependencies. The `define` function is used to define named or unnamed modules based on the following signature:

```
define(
  module_id /*optional*/,
  [dependencies] /*optional*/,
  definition function /*function for instantiating the module or
    object*/
);
```

You can add a module without dependencies as follows:

```
define(
{
  add: function(x, y){
    return x + y;
  }
});
```

The following snippet shows you a module that depends on two other modules:

```
define( "math",
    //dependency on these two modules
    ["sum", "multiply"],
    // module definition function
    // dependencies (foo and bar) are mapped to function parameters
    function ( sum, multiply ) {
        // return a value that defines the module export
        // (that is, the functionality we want to expose for consumption)

        // create your module here
        var math = {
          demo : function () {
            console.log(sum.calculate(1,2));
            console.log(multiply.calculate(1,2));
          }
        };
    return math;
});
```

The `require` module is used as follows:

```
require(["math","draw"], function ( math,draw ) {
  draw.2DRender(math.pi);
});
```

RequireJS (`http://requirejs.org/docs/whyamd.html`) is one of the module loaders that implements AMD.

ES6 modules

Two separate module systems and different module loaders can be a bit intimidating. ES6 tries to solve this. ES6 has a proposed module specification that tries to keep the good aspects of both the CommonJS and AMD module patterns. The syntax of ES6 modules is similar to CommonJS and the ES6 modules support asynchronous loading and configurable module loading:

```
//json_processor.js
function processJSON(url) {
  ...
}
export function getSiteContent(url) {
  return processJSON(url);
}
//main.js
import { getSiteContent } from "json_processor.js";
content=getSiteContent("http://google.com/");
```

ES6 export lets you export a function or variable in a way similar to CommonJS. In the code where you want to use this imported function, you use the `import` keyword to specify from where you want the dependency to be imported. Once the dependency is imported, it can be used as a member of the program. We will discuss in later chapters how you can use ES6 in environments where ES6 is not supported.

The factory pattern

The factory pattern is another popular object creation pattern. It does not require the usage of constructors. This pattern provides an interface to create objects. Based on the type passed to the factory, that particular type of object is created by the factory. A common implementation of this pattern is usually using a class or static method of a class. The purposes of such a class or method are as follows:

- It abstracts out repetitive operations when creating similar objects
- It allows the consumers of the factory to create objects without knowing the internals of the object creation

Let's take a common example to understand the usage of a factory. Let's say that we have the following:

- A constructor, `CarFactory()`
- A static method in `CarFactory` called `make()` that knows how to create objects of the `car` type
- Specific `car` types such as `CarFactory.SUV`, `CarFactory.Sedan`, and so on

We want to use `CarFactory` as follows:

```
var golf = CarFactory.make('Compact');
var vento = CarFactory.make('Sedan');
var touareg = CarFactory.make('SUV');
```

Here is how you would implement such a factory. The following implementation is fairly standard. We are programmatically calling the constructor function that creates an object of the specified type—`CarFactory[const].prototype = new CarFactory();`.

We are mapping object types to the constructors. There can be variations in how you can go about implementing this pattern:

```
// Factory Constructor
function CarFactory() {}
CarFactory.prototype.info = function() {
   console.log("This car has "+this.doors+" doors and a
     "+this.engine_capacity+" liter engine");
};
// the static factory method
CarFactory.make = function (type) {
  var constr 0= type;
  var car;
  CarFactory[constr].prototype = new CarFactory();
  // create a new instance
  car = new CarFactory[constr]();
  return car;
};

CarFactory.Compact = function () {
  this.doors = 4;
  this.engine_capacity = 2;
};
```

```
CarFactory.Sedan = function () {
  this.doors = 2;
  this.engine_capacity = 2;
};
CarFactory.SUV = function () {
  this.doors = 4;
  this.engine_capacity = 6;
};
  var golf = CarFactory.make('Compact');
  var vento = CarFactory.make('Sedan');
  var touareg = CarFactory.make('SUV');
  golf.info(); //"This car has 4 doors and a 2 liter engine"
```

We suggest that you try this example in JS Bin and understand the concept by actually writing its code.

The mixin pattern

Mixins help in significantly reducing functional repetition in our code and help in function reuse. We can move this shared functionality to a mixin and reduce duplication of shared behavior. You can then focus on building the actual functionality and not keep repeating the shared behavior. Let's consider the following example. We want to create a custom logger that can be used by any object instance. The logger will become a functionality shared across objects that want to use/extend the mixin:

```
var _ = require('underscore');
//Shared functionality encapsulated into a CustomLogger
var logger = (function () {
  var CustomLogger = {
    log: function (message) {
      console.log(message);
    }
  };
  return CustomLogger;
}());

//An object that will need the custom logger to log system
  specific logs
var Server = (function (Logger) {
  var CustomServer = function () {
    this.init = function () {
      this.log("Initializing Server...");
    };
```

```
    };

    // This copies/extends the members of the 'CustomLogger' into
      'CustomServer'
    _.extend(CustomServer.prototype, Logger);
    return CustomServer;
}(logger));


(new Server()).init(); //Initializing Server...
```

In this example, we are using `_.extend` from **Underscore.js**—we discussed this function in the previous chapter. This function is used to copy all the properties from the source (`Logger`) to the destination (`CustomServer.prototype`). As you can observe in this example, we are creating a shared `CustomLogger` object that is intended to be used by any object instance needing its functionality. One such object is `CustomServer`—in its `init()` method, we call this custom logger's `log()` method. This method is available to `CustomServer` because we are extending `CustomLogger` via Underscore's `extend()`. We are dynamically adding functionality of a mixin to the consumer object. It is important to understand the distinction between mixins and inheritance. When you have shared functionality across multiple objects and class hierarchies, you can use mixins. If you have shared functionality along a single class hierarchy, you can use inheritance. In prototypical inheritance, when you inherit from a prototype, any change to the prototype affects everything that inherits the prototype. If you do not want this to happen, you can use mixins.

The decorator pattern

The primary idea behind the decorator pattern is that you start your design with a plain object, which has some basic functionality. As the design evolves, you can use existing decorators to enhance your plain object. This is a very popular pattern in the OO world and especially in Java. Let's take an example of `BasicServer`—a server with very basic functionality. This basic functionality can be decorated to serve specific purposes. We can have two different cases where this server can serve both PHP and Node.js and serve them on different ports. These different functionality are decorated to the basic server:

```
var phpServer = new BasicServer();
phpServer = phpServer.decorate('reverseProxy');
phpServer = phpServer.decorate('servePHP');
phpServer = phpServer.decorate('80');
phpServer = phpServer.decorate('serveStaticAssets');
phpServer.init();
```

The Node.js server will have something as follows:

```
var nodeServer = new BasicServer();
nodeServer = nodeServer.decorate('serveNode');
nodeServer = nodeServer.decorate('3000');
nodeServer.init();
```

There are several ways in which the decorator pattern is implemented in JavaScript. We will discuss a method where the pattern is implemented by a list and does not rely on inheritance or method call chain:

```
//Implement BasicServer that does the bare minimum
function BasicServer() {
  this.pid = 1;
  console.log("Initializing basic Server");
  this.decorators_list = []; //Empty list of decorators
}
//List of all decorators
BasicServer.decorators = {};


//Add each decorator to the list of BasicServer's decorators
//Each decorator in this list will be applied on the BasicServer
  instance
BasicServer.decorators.reverseProxy = {
  init: function(pid) {
    console.log("Started Reverse Proxy");
    return pid + 1;
  }
};
BasicServer.decorators.servePHP = {
  init: function(pid) {
    console.log("Started serving PHP");
    return pid + 1;
  }
};
BasicServer.decorators.serveNode = {
  init: function(pid) {
    console.log("Started serving Node");
    return pid + 1;
  }
};
```

```
//Push the decorator to this list everytime decorate() is called
BasicServer.prototype.decorate = function(decorator) {
  this.decorators_list.push(decorator);
};
//init() method looks through all the applied decorators on
  BasicServer
//and executes init() method on all of them
BasicServer.prototype.init = function () {
  var running_processes = 0;
  var pid = this.pid;
  for (i = 0; i < this.decorators_list.length; i += 1) {
    decorator_name = this.decorators_list[i];
    running_processes =
      BasicServer.decorators[decorator_name].init(pid);
  }
  return running_processes;
};

//Create server to serve PHP
var phpServer = new BasicServer();
phpServer.decorate('reverseProxy');
phpServer.decorate('servePHP');
total_processes = phpServer.init();
console.log(total_processes);

//Create server to serve Node
var nodeServer = new BasicServer();
nodeServer.decorate('serveNode');
nodeServer.init();
total_processes = phpServer.init();
console.log(total_processes);
```

`BasicServer.decorate()` and `BasicServer.init()` are the two methods where the real stuff happens. We push all decorators being applied to the list of decorators for `BasicServer`. In the `init()` method, we execute or apply each decorator's `init()` method from this list of decorators. This is a cleaner approach to decorator patterns that does not use inheritance. This method was described by Stoyan Stefanov in his book, *JavaScript Patterns, O'Reilly Media*, and has gained prominence among JavaScript developers due to its simplicity.

The observer pattern

Let's first see the language-agnostic definition of the observer pattern. The GOF book, *Design Patterns: Elements of Reusable Object-Oriented Software*, defines the observer pattern as follows:

One or more observers are interested in the state of a subject and register their interest with the subject by attaching themselves. When something changes in our subject that the observer may be interested in, a notify message is sent which calls the update method in each observer. When the observer is no longer interested in the subject's state, they can simply detach themselves.

In the observer design pattern, the subject keeps a list of objects depending on it (called observers) and notifies them when the state changes. The subject uses a broadcast to the observers to inform them of the change. Observers can remove themselves from the list once they no longer wish to be notified. Based on this understanding, we can define the participants in this pattern:

- **Subject**: This keeps the list of observers and has methods to add, remove, and update observers
- **Observer**: This provides an interface for objects that need to be notified when the subject's state changes

Let's create a subject that can add, remove, and notify observers:

```
var Subject = ( function(  ) {
  function Subject() {
    this.observer_list = [];
  }
  // this method will handle adding observers to the internal list
  Subject.prototype.add_observer = function ( obj ) {
    console.log( 'Added observer' );
    this.observer_list.push( obj );
  };
  Subject.prototype.remove_observer = function ( obj ) {
    for( var i = 0; i < this.observer_list.length; i++ ) {
      if( this.observer_list[ i ] === obj ) {
        this.observer_list.splice( i, 1 );
        console.log( 'Removed Observer' );
      }
    }
  };
```

```
      Subject.prototype.notify = function () {
        var args = Array.prototype.slice.call( arguments, 0 );
        for( var i = 0; i<this.observer_list.length; i++ ) {
          this.observer_list[i].update(args);
        }
      };
      return Subject;
    })();
```

This is a fairly straightforward implementation of a `Subject`. The important fact about the `notify()` method is the way in which all the observer objects' `update()` methods are called to broadcast the update.

Now let's define a simple object that creates random tweets. This object is providing an interface to add and remove observers to the `Subject` via `addObserver()` and `removeObserver()` methods. It also calls the `notify()` method of `Subject` with the newly fetched tweet. When this happens, all the observers will broadcast that the new tweet has been updated with the new tweet being passed as the parameter:

```
    function Tweeter() {
      var subject = new Subject();
      this.addObserver = function ( observer ) {
        subject.add_observer( observer );
      };
      this.removeObserver = function (observer) {
        subject.remove_observer(observer);
      };
      this.fetchTweets = function fetchTweets() {
        // tweet
        var tweet = {
          tweet: "This is one nice observer"
        };
        // notify our observers of the stock change
        subject.notify( tweet );
      };
    }
```

Let's now add two observers:

```
    var TweetUpdater = {
      update : function() {
        console.log( 'Updated Tweet - ', arguments );
      }
    };
```

```
var TweetFollower = {
  update : function() {
    console.log( '"Following this tweet -  ', arguments );
  }
};
```

Both these observers will have one `update()` method that will be called by the
`Subject.notify()` method. Now we can actually add these observers to the
`Subject` via Tweeter's interface:

```
var tweetApp = new Tweeter();
tweetApp.addObserver( TweetUpdater );
tweetApp.addObserver( TweetFollower );
tweetApp.fetchTweets();
tweetApp.removeObserver(TweetUpdater);
tweetApp.removeObserver(TweetFollower);
```

This will result in the following output:

```
Added observer
Added observer
Updated Tweet -   { '0': [ { tweet: 'This is one nice observer' } ] }
"Following this tweet -  { '0': [ { tweet: 'This is one nice
observer' } ] }
Removed Observer
Removed Observer
```

This is a basic implementation to illustrate the idea of the observer pattern.

JavaScript Model-View-* patterns

Model-View-Controller (MVC), **Model-View-Presenter (MVP)**, and **Model-View-
ViewModel (MVVM)** have been popular with server applications, but in recent
years JavaScript applications are also using these patterns to structure and manage
large projects. Many JavaScript frameworks have emerged that support **MV***
patterns. We will discuss a few examples using **Backbone.js**.

Model-View-Controller

MVC is a popular structural pattern where the idea is to divide an application into
three parts so as to separate the internal representations of information from the
presentation layer. MVC consists of components. The model is the application object,
view is the presentation of the underlying model object, and controller handles the
way in which the user interface behaves, depending on the user interactions.

Models

Models are constructs that represent data in the applications. They are agnostic of the user interface or routing logic. Changes to models are typically notified to the view layer by following the observer design pattern. Models may also contain code to validate, create, or delete data. The ability to automatically notify the views to react when the data is changed makes frameworks such as Backbone.js, **Amber.js**, and others very useful in building MV* applications. The following example shows you a typical Backbone model:

```
var EmployeeModel = Backbone.Model.extend({
  url: '/employee/1',
  defaults: {
    id: 1,
    name: 'John Doe',
    occupation: null
  }
  initialize: function() {
  }
}); var JohnDoe = new EmployeeModel();
```

This model structure may vary between different frameworks but they usually have certain commonalities in them. In most real-world applications, you would want your model to be persisted to an in-memory store or database.

Views

Views are the visual representations of your model. Usually, the state of the model is processed, filtered, or massaged before it is presented to the view layer. In JavaScript, views are responsible for rendering and manipulating DOM elements. Views observe models and get notified when there is a change in the model. When the user interacts with the view, certain attributes of the model are changed via the view layer (usually via controllers). In JavaScript frameworks such as Backbone, the views are created using template engines such as **Handlebar.js** (http://handlebarsjs.com/) or **mustache.js** (https://mustache.github.io/). These templates themselves are not views. They observe models and keep the view state updated based on these changes. Let's see an example of a view defined in Handlebar:

```
<li class="employee_photo">
  <h2>{{title}}</h2>
  <img class="emp_headshot_small" src="{{src}}"/>
  <div class="employee_details">
    {{employee_details}}
  </div>
</li>
```

Views such as the preceding example contain markup tags containing template variables. These variables are delimited via a custom syntax. For example, template variables are delimited using {{ }} in Handlebar.js. Frameworks typically transmit data in JSON format. How the view is populated from the model is handled transparently by the framework.

Controllers

Controllers act as a layer between models and views and are responsible for updating the model when the user changes the view attributes. Most JavaScript frameworks deviate from the classical definition of a controller. For example, Backbone does not have a concept called controller; they have something called a **router** that is responsible to handle routing logic. You can think of a combination of the view and router as a controller because a lot of the logic to synchronize models and views is done within the view itself. A typical Backbone router would look as follows:

```
var EmployeeRouter = Backbone.Router.extend({
  routes: { "employee/:id": "route" },
  route: function( id ) {
    ...view render logic...
  }
});
```

The Model-View-Presenter pattern

Model-View-Presenter is a variation of the original MVC pattern that we discussed previously. Both MVC and MVP target the separation of concerns but they are different on many fundamental aspects. The presenter in MVP has the necessary logic for the view. Any invocation from the view gets delegated to the presenter. The presenter also observes the model and updates the views when the model updates. Many authors take the view that because the presenter binds the model with views, it also performs the role of a traditional controller. There are various implementations of MVP and there are no frameworks that offer classical MVP out of the box. In implementations of MVP, the following are the primary differences that separate MVP from MVC:

- The view has no reference to the model
- The presenter has a reference to the model and is responsible for updating the view when the model changes

MVP is generally implemented in two flavors:

- Passive view: The view is as naïve as possible and all the business logic is within the presenter. For example, a plain Handlebars template can be seen as a passive view.

- Supervising controller: Views mostly contain declarative logic. A presenter takes over when the simple declarative logic in the view is insufficient.

The following figure depicts MVP architecture:

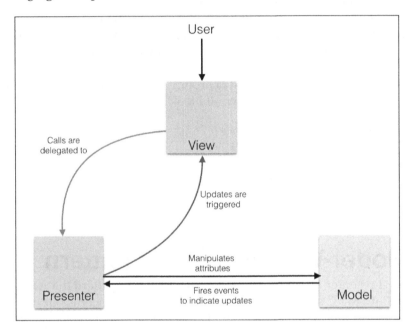

Model-View-ViewModel

MVVM was originally coined by Microsoft for use with **Windows Presentation Foundation (WPF)** and **Silverlight**. MVVM is a variation of MVC and MVP and further tries to separate the user interface (view) from the business model and application behavior. MVVM creates a new model layer in addition to the domain model that we discussed in MVC and MVP. This model layer adds properties as an interface for the view. Let's say that we have a checkbox on the UI. The state of the checkbox is captured in an IsChecked property. In MVP, the view will have this property and the presenter will set it. However, in MVVM, the presenter will have the IsChecked property and the view is responsible for syncing with it. Now that the presenter is not really doing the job of a classical presenter, it's renamed as ViewModel:

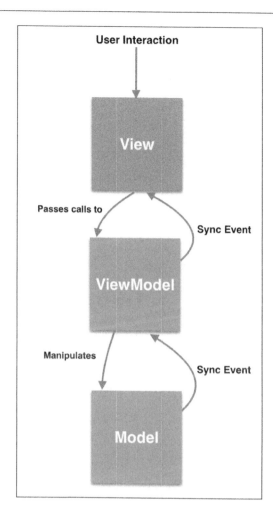

Implementation details of these approaches are dependent on the problem that we are trying to solve and the framework that we use.

Summary

While building large applications, we see certain problem patterns repeating over and over. These patterns have well-defined solutions that can be reused to build a robust solution. In this chapter, we discussed some of the important patterns and ideas around these patterns. Most modern JavaScript applications use these patterns. It is rare to see a large-scale system built without implementing modules, decorators, factories, or MV* patterns. These are foundational ideas that we discussed in this chapter. We will discuss various testing and debugging techniques in the next chapter.

6
Testing and Debugging

As you write JavaScript applications, you will soon realize that having a sound testing strategy is indispensable. In fact, not writing enough tests is almost always a bad idea. It is essential to cover all the non-trivial functionality of your code to make sure of the following points:

- The existing code behaves as per the specifications
- Any new code does not break the behavior defined by the specifications

Both these points are very important. Many engineers consider only the first point the sole reason to cover your code with enough tests. The most obvious advantage of test coverage is to really make sure that the code being pushed to the production system is mostly error-free. Writing test cases to smartly cover the maximum functional areas of the code generally gives you a good indication about the overall quality of the code. There should be no arguments or compromises around this point. It is unfortunate though that many production systems are still bereft of adequate code coverage. It is very important to build an engineering culture where developers think about writing tests as much as they think about writing code.

The second point is even more important. Legacy systems are usually very difficult to manage. When you are working on code written either by someone else or a large distributed team, it is fairly easy to introduce bugs and break things. Even the best engineers make mistakes. When you are working on a large code base that you are unfamiliar with and if there is no sound test coverage to help you, you will introduce bugs. As you won't have the confidence in the changes that you are making (because there are no test cases to confirm your changes), your code releases will be shaky, slow, and obviously full of hidden bugs.

You will refrain from refactoring or optimizing your code because you won't really be sure what changes to the code base would potentially break something (again, because there are no test cases to confirm your changes)—all this is a vicious circle. It's like a civil engineer saying, "though I have constructed this bridge, I have no confidence in the quality of the construction. It may collapse immediately or never." Though this may sound like an exaggeration, I have seen a lot of high impact production code being pushed with no test coverage. This is risky and should be avoided. When you are writing enough test cases to cover majority of your functional code and when you make a change to these pieces, you immediately realize if there is a problem with this new change. If your changes make the test case fail, you realize the problem. If your refactoring breaks the test scenario, you realize the problem—all this happens much before the code is pushed to production.

In recent years, ideas such as test-driven development and self-testing code are gaining prominence, especially in **agile methodology**. These are fundamentally sound ideas and will help you write robust code—code that you are confident of. We will discuss all these ideas in this chapter. You will understand how to write good test cases in modern JavaScript. We will also look at several tools and methods to debug your code. JavaScript has been traditionally a bit difficult to test and debug primarily due to lack of tools, but modern tools make both of these easy and natural.

Unit testing

When we talk about test cases, we mostly mean **unit tests**. It is incorrect to assume that the unit that we want to test is always a function. The unit (or unit of work) is a logical unit that constitutes a single behavior. This unit should be able to be invoked via a public interface and should be testable independently.

Thus, a unit test performs the following functions:

- It tests a single logical function
- It can be run without a specific order of execution
- It takes care of its own dependencies and mock data
- It always returns the same result for the same input
- It should be self-explanatory, maintainable, and readable

Martin Fowler advocates the **test pyramid** (http://martinfowler.com/bliki/TestPyramid.html) strategy to make sure that we have a high number of unit tests to ensure maximum code coverage. The test pyramid says that you should write many more low-level unit tests than higher level integration and UI tests.

There are two important testing strategies that we will discuss in this chapter.

Test-driven development

Test-driven development (TDD) has gained a lot of prominence in the last few years. The concept was first proposed as part of the **Extreme Programming** methodology. The idea is to have short repetitive development cycles where the focus is on writing the test cases first. The cycle looks as follows:

1. Add a test case as per the specifications for a specific unit of code.
2. Run the existing suite of test cases to see if the new test case that you wrote fails—it should (because there is no code for this unit yet). This step ensures that the current test harness works well.
3. Write the code that serves mainly to confirm the test case. This code is not optimized or refactored or even entirely correct. However, this is fine at the moment.
4. Rerun the tests and see if all the test cases pass. After this step, you will be confident that the new code is not breaking anything.
5. Refactor the code to make sure that you are optimizing the unit and handling all corner cases.

These steps are repeated for all the new code that you add. This is an elegant strategy that works really well for the agile methodology. TDD will be successful only if the testable units of code are small and confirm only to the test case and nothing more. It is important to write small, modular, and precise code units that have input and output confirming the test case.

Behavior-driven development

A very common problem while trying to follow TDD is vocabulary and the definition of *correctness*. BDD tries to introduce a *ubiquitous language* while writing the test cases when you are following TDD. This language makes sure that both the business and engineering teams are talking about the same thing.

We will use **Jasmine** as the primary BDD framework and explore various testing strategies.

 You can install Jasmine by downloading the standalone package from `https://github.com/jasmine/jasmine/releases/download/ v2.3.4/jasmine-standalone-2.3.4.zip`.

When you unzip this package, you will have the following directory structure:

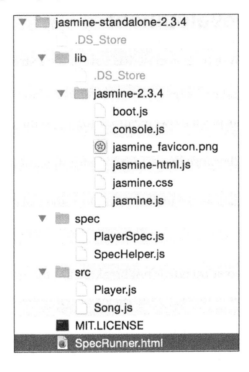

The `lib` directory contains the JavaScript files that you need in your project to start writing Jasmine test cases. If you open `SpecRunner.html`, you will find the following JavaScript files included in it:

```html
<script src="lib/jasmine-2.3.4/jasmine.js"></script>
<script src="lib/jasmine-2.3.4/jasmine-html.js"></script>
<script src="lib/jasmine-2.3.4/boot.js"></script>

<!-- include source files here... -->
<script src="src/Player.js"></script>
```

```
<script src="src/Song.js"></script>
<!-- include spec files here... -->
<script src="spec/SpecHelper.js"></script>
<script src="spec/PlayerSpec.js"></script>
```

The first three are Jasmine's own framework files. The next section includes the source files that we want to test and the actual test specifications.

Let's experiment with Jasmine with a very ordinary example. Create a bigfatjavascriptcode.js file and place it in the src/ directory. We will test the following function:

```
function capitalizeName(name){
    return name.toUpperCase();
}
```

This is a simple function that does one single thing. It receives a string and returns a capitalized string. We will test various scenarios around this function. This is the unit of code that we discussed earlier.

Next, create the test specifications. Create one JavaScript file, test.spec.js, and place it in the spec/ directory. The file should contain the following. You will need to add the following two lines to SpecRunner.html:

```
<script src="src/bigfatjavascriptcode.js"></script>
<script src="spec/test.spec.js"></script>
```

The order of this inclusion does not matter. When we run SpecRunner.html, you will see something as follows:

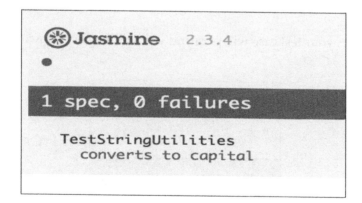

This is the Jasmine report that shows the details about the number of tests that were executed and the count of failures and successes. Now, let's make the test case fail. We want to test a case where an undefined variable is passed to the function. Add one more test case as follows:

```
it("can handle undefined", function() {
  var str= undefined;
  expect(capitalizeName(str)).toEqual(undefined);
});
```

Now, when you run `SpecRunner.html`, you will see the following result:

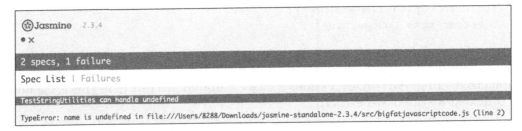

As you can see, the failure is displayed for this test case in a detailed error stack. Now, we go about fixing this. In your original JavaScript code, we can handle an undefined condition as follows:

```
function capitalizeName(name){
  if(name){
    return name.toUpperCase();
  }
}
```

With this change, your test case will pass and you will see the following in the Jasmine report:

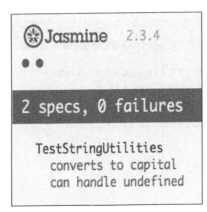

This is very similar to what a test-driven development would look. You write test cases, you then fill in the necessary code to confirm to the specifications, and rerun the test suite. Let's understand the structure of the Jasmine tests.

Our test specification looks as follows:

```
describe("TestStringUtilities", function() {
  it("converts to capital", function() {
    var str = "albert";
    expect(capitalizeName(str)).toEqual("ALBERT");
  });
  it("can handle undefined", function() {
    var str= undefined;
    expect(capitalizeName(str)).toEqual(undefined);
  });
});
```

The `describe("TestStringUtilities"` is a test suite. The name of the test suite should describe the unit of code that we are testing – this can be a function or group of related functionality. In the specifications, you call the global Jasmine `it` function to which you pass the title of the specification and test function used by the test case. This function is the actual test case. You can catch one or more assertions or the general expectations using the `expect` function. When all expectations are `true`, your specification is passed. You can write any valid JavaScript code in the `describe` and `it` functions. The values that you verify as part of the expectations are matched using a matcher. In our example, `toEqual()` is the matcher that matches two values for equality. Jasmine contains a rich set of matches to suit most of the common use cases. Some common matchers supported by Jasmine are as follows:

- `toBe()`: This matcher checks whether two objects being compared are equal. This is the same as the `===` comparison, as shown in the following code:

```
var a = { value: 1};
var b = { value: 1 };

expect(a).toEqual(b);   // success, same as == comparison
expect(b).toBe(b);      // failure, same as === comparison
expect(a).toBe(a);      // success, same as === comparison
```

- not: You can negate a matcher with a `not` prefix. For example, `expect(1).not.toEqual(2);` will negate the match made by `toEqual()`.

- `toContain()`: This checks whether an element is part of an array. This is not an exact object match as `toBe()`. For example, look at the following code:

```
expect([1, 2, 3]).toContain(3);
expect("astronomy is a science").toContain("science");
```

- `toBeDefined()` and `toBeUndefined()`: These two matches are handy to check whether a variable is undefined (or not).

- `toBeNull()`: This checks whether a variable's value is `null`.

- `toBeGreaterThan()` and `toBeLessThan()`: These matchers perform numeric comparisons (they work on strings too):

```
expect(2).toBeGreaterThan(1);
expect(1).toBeLessThan(2);
expect("a").toBeLessThan("b");
```

One interesting feature of Jasmine is the **spies**. When you are writing a large system, it is not possible to make sure that all systems are always available and correct. At the same time, you don't want your unit tests to fail due to a dependency that may be broken or unavailable. To simulate a situation where all dependencies are available for a unit of code that we want to test, we mock these dependencies to always give the response that we expect. Mocking is an important aspect of testing and most testing frameworks provide support for the mocking. Jasmine allows mocking using a feature called a spy. Jasmine spies essentially stub the functions that we may not have ready; at the time of writing the test case but as part of the functionality, we need to track that we are executing these dependencies and not ignoring them. Consider the following example:

```
describe("mocking configurator", function() {
  var configurator = null;
  var responseJSON = {};

  beforeEach(function() {
    configurator = {
      submitPOSTRequest: function(payload) {
        //This is a mock service that will eventually be replaced
        //by a real service
        console.log(payload);
        return {"status": "200"};
      }
    };
    spyOn(configurator,
      'submitPOSTRequest').and.returnValue({"status": "200"});
    configurator.submitPOSTRequest({
```

```
       "port":"8000",
       "client-encoding":"UTF-8"
    });
  });

  it("the spy was called", function() {
    expect(configurator.submitPOSTRequest).toHaveBeenCalled();
  });

  it("the arguments of the spy's call are tracked", function() {
    expect(configurator.submitPOSTRequest).toHaveBeenCalledWith({"port
":"8000","client-encoding":"UTF-8"});
  });
});
```

In this example, while we are writing this test case, we either don't have the real implementation of the `configurator.submitPOSTRequest()` dependency or someone is fixing this particular dependency. In any case, we don't have it available. For our test to work, we need to mock it. Jasmine spies allow us to replace a function with its mock and track its execution.

In this case, we need to ensure that we called the dependency. When the actual dependency is ready, we will revisit this test case to make sure that it fits the specifications, but at this time, all that we need to ensure is that the dependency is called. The Jasmine `tohaveBeenCalled()` function lets us track the execution of a function, which may be a mock. We can use `toHaveBeenCalledWith()` that allows us to determine if the stub function was called with the correct parameters. There are several other interesting scenarios that you can create using Jasmine spies. The scope of this chapter won't permit us to cover them all, but I would encourage you to discover these areas on your own.

> You can refer to the user manual for Jasmine for more information on Jasmine spies at `http://jasmine.github.io/2.0/introduction.html`.

Mocha, Chai, and Sinon

Though Jasmine is the most prominent JavaScript testing framework, **Mocha** and **Chai** are gaining prominence in the Node.js environment. Mocha is the testing framework used to describe and run test cases. Chai is the assertion library supported by Mocha. **Sinon.JS** comes in handy while creating mocks and stubs for your tests. We won't discuss these frameworks in this book, but experience on Jasmine will be handy if you want to experiment with these frameworks.

JavaScript debugging

If you are not a completely new programmer, I am sure you must have spent some amount of time debugging your or someone else's code. Debugging is almost like an art form. Every language has different methods and challenges around debugging. JavaScript has traditionally been a difficult language to debug. I have personally spent days and nights of misery trying to debug badly-written JavaScript code using `alert()` functions. Fortunately, modern browsers such as Mozilla Firefox and Google Chrome have excellent developer tools to help debug JavaScript in the browser. There are IDEs like **IntelliJ WebStorm** with great debugging support for JavaScript and Node.js. In this chapter, we will focus primarily on Google Chrome's built-in developer tool. Firefox also supports the Firebug extension and has excellent built-in developer tools, but as they behave more or less the same as Google Chrome's **Developer Tools** (**DevTools**), we will discuss common debugging approaches that work in both of these tools.

Before we talk about the specific debugging techniques, let's understand the type of errors that we would be interested in while we try to debug our code.

Syntax errors

When your code has something that does not confirm to the JavaScript language grammar, the interpreter rejects this piece of code. These are easy to catch if your IDE is helping you with syntax checking. Most modern IDEs help with these errors. Earlier, we discussed the usefulness of the tools such as **JSLint** and **JSHint** around catching syntax issues with your code. They analyze the code and flag errors in the syntax. JSHint output can be very illuminating. For example, the following output shows up so many things that we can change in the code. This snippet is from one of my existing projects:

```
temp git:(dev_branch) ⊠ jshint test.js
test.js: line 1, col 1, Use the function form of "use strict".
test.js: line 4, col 1, 'destructuring expression' is available in
   ES6 (use esnext option) or Mozilla JS extensions (use moz).
test.js: line 44, col 70, 'arrow function syntax (=>)' is only
   available in ES6 (use esnext option).
test.js: line 61, col 33, 'arrow function syntax (=>)' is only
   available in ES6 (use esnext option).
test.js: line 200, col 29, Expected ')' to match '(' from line 200
   and instead saw ':'.
test.js: line 200, col 29, 'function closure expressions' is only
   available in Mozilla JavaScript extensions (use moz option).
test.js: line 200, col 37, Expected '}' to match '{' from line 36
   and instead saw ')'.
```

```
test.js: line 200, col 39, Expected ')' and instead saw '{'.
test.js: line 200, col 40, Missing semicolon.
```

Using strict

We briefly discussed the **strict** mode in earlier chapters. The strict mode in JavaScript flags or eliminates some of the JavaScript silent errors. Rather than silently failing, the strict mode makes these failures throw errors instead. The strict mode also helps in converting mistakes to actual errors. There are two ways of enforcing the strict mode. If you want the strict mode for the entire script, you can just add the `use strict` statement as the first line of your JavaScript program. If you want a specific function to conform with the strict mode, you can add the directive as the first line of a function:

```
function strictFn(){
// This line makes EVERYTHING under this strict mode
'use strict';
...
function nestedStrictFn() {
//Everything in this function is also nested
...
}
}
```

Runtime exceptions

These errors appear when you execute the code and try to refer to an undefined variable or process a null. When a runtime exception occurs, any code after that particular line (which caused the exception) does not get executed. It is essential to handle such exceptional scenarios correctly in the code. While exception handling can help prevent crashes, they also aid in debugging. You can wrap the code that *may* encounter a runtime exception in a `try{ }` block. When any code in this block generates a runtime exception, a corresponding handler captures it. The handler is defined by a `catch(exception){}` block. Let's clarify this using an example:

```
try {
  var a = doesnotexist; // throws a runtime exception
} catch(e) {
  console.log(e.message);  //handle the exception
  //prints - "doesnotexist is not defined"
}
```

In this example, the `var a = doesnotexist;` line tries to assign an undefined variable, `doesnotexist`, to another variable, `a`. This causes a runtime exception. When we wrap this problematic code in the `try{}` `catch(){}` block and when the exception occurs (or is thrown), the execution stops in the `try{}` block and goes directly to the `catch()` `{}` handler. The `catch` handler is responsible for handling the exceptional scenario. In this case, we are displaying the error message on the console for debugging purposes. You can explicitly throw an exception to trigger an unhandled scenario in the code. Consider the following example:

```
function engageGear(gear){
  if(gear==="R"){ console.log ("Reversing");}
  if(gear==="D"){ console.log ("Driving");}
  if(gear==="N"){ console.log ("Neutral/Parking");}
  throw new Error("Invalid Gear State");
}
try
{
  engageGear("R");   //Reversing
  engageGear("P");   //Invalid Gear State
}
catch(e){
  console.log(e.message);
}
```

In this example, we are handling valid states of a gear shift (R, N, and D), but when we receive an invalid state, we are explicitly throwing an exception clearly stating the reason. When we call the function that we think may throw an exception, we wrap the code in the `try{}` block and attach a `catch(){}` handler with it. When the exception is caught by the `catch()` block, we handle the exceptional condition appropriately.

Console.log and asserts

Displaying the state of execution on the console can be very useful while debugging. However, modern developer tools allow you to put breakpoints and halt execution to inspect a particular value during runtime. You can quickly detect small issues by logging some variable state on the console.

With these concepts, let's see how we can use Chrome Developer Tools to debug JavaScript code.

Chrome DevTools

You can start Chrome DevTools by navigating to menu | **More tools** | **Developer Tools**:

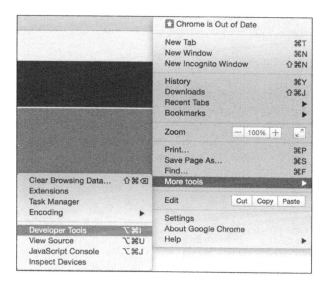

Chrome DevTools opens up on the lower pane of your browser and has a bunch of very useful sections:

The **Elements** panel helps you inspect and monitor the DOM tree and associated style sheet for each of these components.

The **Network** panel is useful to understand network activity. For example, you can monitor the resources being downloaded over the network in real time.

The most important pane for us is the **Sources** pane. This pane is where the JavaScript source and debugger are displayed. Let's create a sample HTML with the following content:

```html
<!DOCTYPE html>
<html>
<head>
  <meta charset="utf-8">
  <title>This test</title>
  <script type="text/javascript">
  function engageGear(gear){
    if(gear==="R"){ console.log ("Reversing");}
    if(gear==="D"){ console.log ("Driving");}
    if(gear==="N"){ console.log ("Neutral/Parking");}
    throw new Error("Invalid Gear State");
  }
  try
  {
    engageGear("R");   //Reversing
    engageGear("P");   //Invalid Gear State
  }
  catch(e){
    console.log(e.message);
  }
  </script>
</head>
<body>
</body>
</html>
```

Save this HTML file and open it in Google Chrome. Open DevTools in the browser and you will see the following screen:

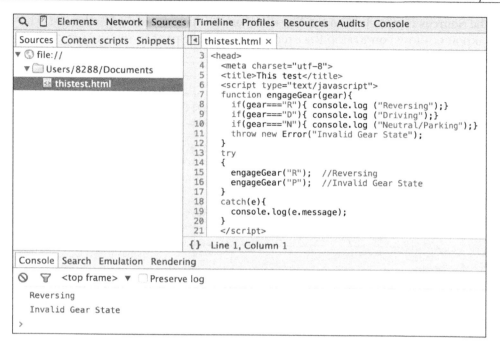

This is the view of the **Sources** panel. You can see the HTML and embedded JavaScript source in this panel. You can see the **Console** window as well. You can see that the file is executed and output is displayed in the **Console**.

On the right-hand side, you will see the debugger window:

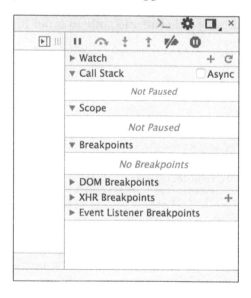

In the **Sources** panel, click on the line numbers **8** and **15** to add a breakpoint. The breakpoints allow you to stop the execution of the script at the specified point:

```
4    <meta charset="utf-8">
5    <title>This test</title>
6    <script type="text/javascript">
7    function engageGear(gear){
8        if(gear==="R"){ console.log ("Reversi
9        if(gear==="D"){ console.log ("Driving
10       if(gear==="N"){ console.log ("Neutral
11       throw new Error("Invalid Gear State")
12   }
13   try
14   {
15       engageGear("R");   //Reversing
16       engageGear("P");   //Invalid Gear Stat
17   }
```

In the debugging pane, you can see all the existing breakpoints:

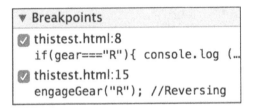

```
▼ Breakpoints
☑ thistest.html:8
     if(gear==="R"){ console.log (…
☑ thistest.html:15
     engageGear("R"); //Reversing
```

Now, when you rerun the same page, you will see that the execution stops at the debug point. One very useful technique is to inject code during the debugging phase. While the debugger is running, you can add code in order to help you understand the state of the code better:

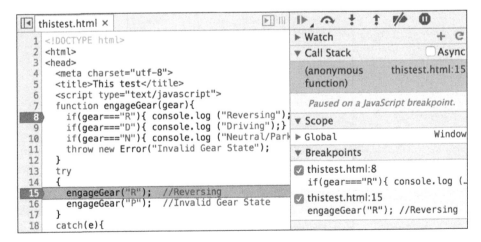

This window now has all the action. You can see that the execution is paused on line **15**. In the debug window, you can see which breakpoint is being triggered. You can see the **Call Stack** also. You can resume execution in several ways. The debug command window has a bunch of actions:

You can resume execution (which will execute until the next breakpoint) by clicking on the 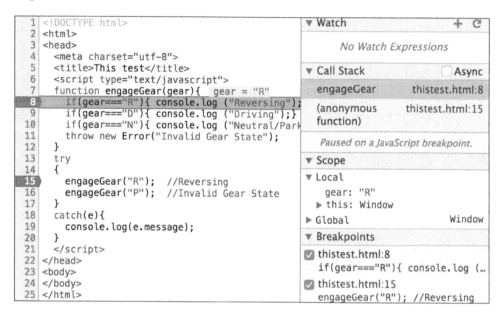 button. When you do this, the execution continues until the next breakpoint is encountered. In our case, we halt at line **8**:

```
 1  <!DOCTYPE html>
 2  <html>
 3  <head>
 4    <meta charset="utf-8">
 5    <title>This test</title>
 6    <script type="text/javascript">
 7    function engageGear(gear){    gear = "R"
 8      if(gear==="R"){ console.log ("Reversing");
 9      if(gear==="D"){ console.log ("Driving");}
10      if(gear==="N"){ console.log ("Neutral/Park
11      throw new Error("Invalid Gear State");
12    }
13    try
14    {
15      engageGear("R");   //Reversing
16      engageGear("P");   //Invalid Gear State
17    }
18    catch(e){
19      console.log(e.message);
20    }
21    </script>
22  </head>
23  <body>
24  </body>
25  </html>
```

▼ Watch   + ⟳

No Watch Expressions

▼ Call Stack   ☐ Async

engageGear   thistest.html:8

(anonymous   thistest.html:15
function)

Paused on a JavaScript breakpoint.

▼ Scope

▼ Local
  gear: "R"
  ▶ this: Window
▶ Global   Window

▼ Breakpoints

☑ thistest.html:8
  if(gear==="R"){ console.log (…

☑ thistest.html:15
  engageGear("R"); //Reversing

You can observe that the **Call Stack** window shows you how we arrived at line **8**. The **Scope** panel shows the **Local** scope where you can see the variables in the scope when the breakpoint was arrived at. You can also step into or step over the next function.

There are other very useful mechanisms to debug and profile your code using Chrome DevTools. I would suggest you to go experiment with the tool and make it a part of your regular development flow.

Summary

Both the testing and debugging phases are essential to developing robust JavaScript code. TDD and BDD are approaches closely associated with the agile methodology and are widely embraced by the JavaScript developer community. In this chapter, we reviewed the best practices around TDD and usage of Jasmine as the testing framework. We saw various methods of debugging JavaScript using Chrome DevTools. In the next chapter, we will explore the new and exciting world of ES6, DOM manipulation, and cross-browser strategies.

7
ECMAScript 6

So far, we have taken a detailed tour of the JavaScript programming language. I am sure that you must have gained significant insight into the core of the language. What we saw so far was as per the **ECMAScript 5 (ES5)** standards. **ECMAScript 6 (ES6)** or **ECMAScript 2015 (ES2015)** is the latest version of the ECMAScript standard. This standard is evolving and the last round of modifications was done in June, 2015. ES2015 is significant in its scope and the recommendations of ES2015 are being implemented in most JavaScript engines. This is great news. ES6 introduces a huge number of features that add syntactic forms and helpers that enrich the language significantly. The pace at which ECMAScript standards keep evolving makes it a bit difficult for browsers and JavaScript engines to support new features. It is also a practical reality that most programmers have to write code that can be supported by older browsers. The notorious Internet Explorer 6 was once the most widely used browser in the world. To make sure that your code is compatible with the most number of browsers is a daunting task. So, while you want to jump to the next set of awesome ES6 features, you will have to consider the fact that several ES6 features may not be supported by the most popular of browsers or JavaScript frameworks.

This may look like a dire scenario, but things are not that dark. **Node.js** uses the latest version of the V8 engine that supports majority of ES6 features. Facebook's **React** also supports them. Mozilla Firefox and Google Chrome are two of the most used browsers today and they support a majority of ES6 features.

To avoid such pitfalls and unpredictability, certain solutions have been proposed. The most useful among these are polyfills/shims and transpilers.

Shims or polyfills

Polyfills (also known as shims) are patterns to define behavior from a new version in a compatible form supported by an older version of the environment. There's a great collection of ES6 shims called **ES6 shim** (`https://github.com/paulmillr/es6-shim/`); I would highly recommend a study of these shims. From the ES6 shim collection, consider the following example of a shim.

The `Number.isFinite()` method of the ECMAScript 2015 (ES6) standard determines whether the passed value is a finite number. The equivalent shim for it would look something as follows:

```
var numberIsFinite = Number.isFinite || function isFinite(value) {
    return typeof value === 'number' && globalIsFinite(value);
};
```

The shim first checks if the `Number.isFinite()` method is available; if not, it *fills* it up with an implementation. This is a pretty nifty technique to fill in gaps in specifications. Shims are constantly upgraded with newer features and, hence, it is a sound strategy to keep the most updated shims in your project.

> The `endsWith()` polyfill is described in detail at `https://developer.mozilla.org/en-US/docs/Web/JavaScript/Reference/Global_Objects/String/endsWith`. `String.endsWith()` is part of ES6 but can be polyfilled easily for pre-ES6 environments.

Shims, however, cannot polyfill syntactical changes. For this, we can consider transpilers as an option.

Transpilers

Transpiling is a technique that combines both compilation and transformation. The idea is to write ES6-compatible code and use a tool that transpiles this code into a valid and equivalent ES5 code. We will be looking at the most complete and popular transpiler for ES6 called **Babel** (`https://babeljs.io/`).

Babel can be used in various ways. You can install it as a node module and invoke it from the command line or import it as a script in your web page. Babel's setup is exhaustive and well-documented at `https://babeljs.io/docs/setup/`. Babel also has a great **Read-Eval-Print-Loop (REPL)**. We will Babel REPL for most of the examples in this chapter. An in-depth understanding of various ways in which Babel can be used is out of the scope of this book. However, I would urge you to start using Babel as part of your development workflow.

We will cover the most important part of ES6 specifications in this chapter. You should explore all the features of ES6 if possible and make them part of your development workflow.

ES6 syntax changes

ES6 brings in significant syntactic changes to JavaScript. These changes need careful study and some getting used to. In this section, we will study some of the most important syntax changes and see how you can use Babel to start using these newer constructs in your code right away.

Block scoping

We discussed earlier that the variables in JavaScript are function-scoped. Variables created in a nested scope are available to the entire function. Several programming languages provide you with a default block scope where any variable declared within a block of code (usually delimited by {}) is scoped (available) only within this block. To achieve a similar block scope in JavaScript, a prevalent method is to use **immediately-invoked function expressions (IIFE)**. Consider the following example:

```
var a = 1;
(function blockscope(){
    var a = 2;
    console.log(a);    // 2
})();
console.log(a);        // 1
```

Using the IIFE, we are creating a block scope for the a variable. When a variable is declared in the IIFE, its scope is restricted within the function. This is the traditional way of simulating the block scope. ES6 supports block scoping without using IIFEs. In ES6, you can enclose any statement(s) in a block defined by {}. Instead of using var, you can declare a variable using let to define the block scope. The preceding example can be rewritten using ES6 block scopes as follows:

```
"use strict";
var a = 1;
{
  let a = 2;
  console.log( a ); // 2
}
console.log( a ); // 1
```

Using standalone brackets { } may seem unusual in JavaScript, but this convention is fairly common to create a block scope in many languages. The block scope kicks in other constructs such as if { } or for () { } as well.

When you use a block scope in this way, it is generally preferred to put the variable declaration on top of the block. One difference between variables declared using var and let is that variables declared with var are attached to the entire function scope, while variables declared using let are attached to the block scope and they are not initialized until they appear in the block. Hence, you cannot access a variable declared with let earlier than its declaration, whereas with variables declared using var, the ordering doesn't matter:

```
function fooey() {
  console.log(foo); // ReferenceError
  let foo = 5000;
}
```

One specific use of let is in for loops. When we use a variable declared using var in a for loop, it is created in the global or parent scope. We can create a block-scoped variable in the for loop scope by declaring a variable using let. Consider the following example:

```
for (let i = 0; i<5; i++) {
  console.log(i);
}
console.log(i); // i is not defined
```

As i is created using let, it is scoped in the for loop. You can see that the variable is not available outside the scope.

One more use of block scopes in ES6 is the ability to create constants. Using the const keyword, you can create constants in the block scope. Once the value is set, you cannot change the value of such a constant:

```
if(true){
  const a=1;
  console.log(a);
  a=100;  ///"a" is read-only, you will get a TypeError
}
```

A constant has to be initialized while being declared. The same block scope rules apply to functions also. When a function is declared inside a block, it is available only within that scope.

Default parameters

Defaulting is very common. You always set some default value to parameters passed to a function or variables that you initialize. You may have seen code similar to the following:

```
function sum(a,b){
  a = a || 0;
  b = b || 0;
  return (a+b);
}
console.log(sum(9,9)); //18
console.log(sum(9));   //9
```

Here, we are using || (the OR operator) to default variables a and b to 0 if no value was supplied when this function was invoked. With ES6, you have a standard way of defaulting function arguments. The preceding example can be rewritten as follows:

```
function sum(a=0, b=0){
  return (a+b);
}
console.log(sum(9,9)); //18
console.log(sum(9));   //9
```

You can pass any valid expression or function call as part of the default parameter list.

Spread and rest

ES6 has a new operator, ... Based on how it is used, it is called either spread or rest. Let's look at a trivial example:

```
function print(a, b){
  console.log(a,b);
}
print(...[1,2]);  //1,2
```

What's happening here is that when you add ... before an array (or an iterable) it *spreads* the element of the array in individual variables in the function parameters. The a and b function parameters were assigned two values from the array when it was spread out. Extra parameters are ignored while spreading an array:

```
print(...[1,2,3 ]);  //1,2
```

This would still print 1 and 2 because there are only two functional parameters available. Spreads can be used in other places also, such as array assignments:

```
var a = [1,2];
var b = [ 0, ...a, 3 ];
console.log( b ); //[0,1,2,3]
```

There is another use of the ... operator that is the very opposite of the one that we just saw. Instead of spreading the values, the same operator can gather them into one:

```
function print (a,...b){
   console.log(a,b);
}
console.log(print(1,2,3,4,5,6,7));   //1 [2,3,4,5,6,7]
```

In this case, the variable b takes the *rest* of the values. The a variable took the first value as 1 and b took the rest of the values as an array.

Destructuring

If you have worked on a functional language such as **Erlang**, you will relate to the concept of pattern matching. Destructuring in JavaScript is something very similar. Destructuring allows you to bind values to variables using pattern matching. Consider the following example:

```
var [start, end] = [0,5];
for (let i=start; i<end; i++){
   console.log(i);
}
//prints - 0,1,2,3,4
```

We are assigning two variables with the help of array destructuring:

```
var [start, end] = [0,5];
```

As shown in the preceding example, we want the pattern to match when the first value is assigned to the first variable (start) and the second value is assigned to the second variable (end). Consider the following snippet to see how the destructuring of array elements works:

```
function fn() {
   return [1,2,3];
}
var [a,b,c]=fn();
console.log(a,b,c); //1 2 3
```

```
//We can skip one of them
var [d,,f]=fn();
console.log(d,f);    //1 3
//Rest of the values are not used
var [e,] = fn();
console.log(e);      //1
```

Let's discuss how objects' destructuring works. Let's say that you have a function `f` that returns an object as follows:

```
function f() {
   return {
      a: 'a',
      b: 'b',
      c: 'c'
   };
}
```

When we destructure the object being returned by this function, we can use the similar syntax as we saw earlier; the difference is that we use `{}` instead of `[]`:

```
var { a: a, b: b, c: c } = f();
console.log(a,b,c); //a b c
```

Similar to arrays, we use pattern matching to assign variables to their corresponding values returned by the function. There is an even shorter way of writing this if you are using the same variable as the one being matched. The following example would do just fine:

```
var { a,b,c } = f();
```

However, you would mostly be using a different variable name from the one being returned by the function. It is important to remember that the syntax is *source: destination* and not the usual *destination: source*. Carefully observe the following example:

```
//this is target: source - which is incorrect
var { x: a, x: b, x: c } = f();
console.log(x,y,z); //x is undefined, y is undefined z is undefined
//this is source: target - correct
var { a: x, b: y, c: z } = f();
console.log(x,y,z); // a b c
```

This is the opposite of the *target = source* way of assigning values and hence will take some time in getting used to.

Object literals

Object literals are everywhere in JavaScript. You would think that there is no scope of improvement there. However, ES6 wants to improve this too. ES6 introduces several shortcuts to create a concise syntax around object literals:

```
var firstname = "Albert", lastname = "Einstein",
  person = {
    firstname: firstname,
    lastname: lastname
  };
```

If you intend to use the same property name as the variable that you are assigning, you can use the concise property notation of ES6:

```
var firstname = "Albert", lastname = "Einstein",
  person = {
    firstname,
    lastname
  };
```

Similarly, you are assigning functions to properties as follows:

```
var person = {
  getName: function(){
    // ..
  },
  getAge: function(){
    //..
  }
}
```

Instead of the preceding lines, you can say the following:

```
var person = {
  getName(){
    // ..
  },
  getAge(){
    //..
  }
}
```

Template literals

I am sure you have done things such as the following:

```
function SuperLogger(level, clazz, msg){
  console.log(level+": Exception happened in class:"+clazz+" -
    Exception :"+ msg);
}
```

This is a very common way of replacing variable values to form a string literal. ES6 provides you with a new type of string literal using the backtick (`` ` ``) delimiter. You can use string interpolation to put placeholders in a template string literal. The placeholders will be parsed and evaluated.

The preceding example can be rewritten as follows:

```
function SuperLogger(level, clazz, msg){
  console.log(`${level} : Exception happened in class: ${clazz} -
    Exception : {$msg}`);
}
```

We are using `` `` `` around a string literal. Within this literal, any expression of the ${..} form is parsed immediately. This parsing is called interpolation. While parsing, the variable's value replaces the placeholder within ${}. The resulting string is just a normal string with the placeholders replaced with actual variable values.

With string interpolation, you can split a string into multiple lines also, as shown in the following code (very similar to Python):

```
var quote =
`Good night, good night!
Parting is such sweet sorrow,
that I shall say good night
till it be morrow.`;
console.log( quote );
```

You can use function calls or valid JavaScript expressions as part of the string interpolation:

```
function sum(a,b){
  console.log(`The sum seems to be ${a + b}`);
}
sum(1,2); //The sum seems to be 3
```

The final variation of the template strings is called **tagged template string**. The idea is to modify the template string using a function. Consider the following example:

```
function emmy(key, ...values){
   console.log(key);
   console.log(values);
}
let category="Best Movie";
let movie="Adventures in ES6";
emmy`And the award for ${category} goes to ${movie}`;

//["And the award for "," goes to ",""]
//["Best Movie","Adventures in ES6"]
```

The strangest part is when we call the emmy function with the template literal. It's not a traditional function call syntax. We are not writing emmy(); we are just *tagging* the literal with the function. When this function is called, the first argument is an array of all the plain strings (the string between interpolated expressions). The second argument is the array where all the interpolated expressions are evaluated and stored.

Now what this means is that the tag function can actually change the resulting template tag:

```
function priceFilter(s, ...v){
   //Bump up discount
   return s[0]+ (v[0] + 5);
}
let default_discount = 20;
let greeting = priceFilter `Your purchase has a discount of
   ${default_discount} percent`;
console.log(greeting);  //Your purchase has a discount of 25
```

As you can see, we modified the value of the discount in the tag function and returned the modified values.

Maps and Sets

ES6 introduces four new data structures: **Map**, **WeakMap**, **Set**, and **WeakSet**. We discussed earlier that objects are the usual way of creating key-value pairs in JavaScript. The disadvantage of objects is that you cannot use non-string values as keys. The following snippets demonstrate how Maps are created in ES6:

```
let m = new Map();
let s = { 'seq' : 101 };

m.set('1','Albert');
m.set('MAX', 99);
m.set(s,'Einstein');

console.log(m.has('1')); //true
console.log(m.get(s));   //Einstein
console.log(m.size);     //3
m.delete(s);
m.clear();
```

You can initialize the map while declaring it:

```
let m = new Map([
  [ 1, 'Albert' ],
  [ 2, 'Douglas' ],
  [ 3, 'Clive' ],
]);
```

If you want to iterate over the entries in the Map, you can use the `entries()` function that will return you an iterator. You can iterate through all the keys using the `keys()` function and you can iterate through the values of the Map using the `values()` function:

```
let m2 = new Map([
    [ 1, 'Albert' ],
    [ 2, 'Douglas' ],
    [ 3, 'Clive' ],
]);
for (let a of m2.entries()){
  console.log(a);
}
//[1,"Albert"] [2,"Douglas"][3,"Clive"]
for (let a of m2.keys()){
  console.log(a);
} //1 2 3
for (let a of m2.values()){
  console.log(a);
}
//Albert Douglas Clive
```

A variation of JavaScript Maps is a WeakMap—a WeakMap does not prevent its keys from being garbage-collected. Keys for a WeakMap must be objects and the values can be arbitrary values. While a WeakMap behaves in the same way as a normal Map, you cannot iterate through it and you can't clear it. There are reasons behind these restrictions. As the state of the Map is not guaranteed to remain static (keys may get garbage-collected), you cannot ensure correct iteration.

There are not many cases where you may want to use WeakMap. Most uses of a Map can be written using normal Maps.

While Maps allow you to store arbitrary values, Sets are a collection of unique values. Sets have similar methods as Maps; however, `set()` is replaced with `add()`, and the `get()` method does not exist. The reason that the `get()` method is not there is because a Set has unique values, so you are interested in only checking whether the Set contains a value or not. Consider the following example:

```
let x = {'first': 'Albert'};
let s = new Set([1,2,'Sunday',x]);
//console.log(s.has(x));  //true
s.add(300);
//console.log(s);  //[1,2,"Sunday",{"first":"Albert"},300]

for (let a of s.entries()){
  console.log(a);
}
//[1,1]
//[2,2]
//["Sunday","Sunday"]
//[{"first":"Albert"},{"first":"Albert"}]
//[300,300]
for (let a of s.keys()){
  console.log(a);
}
//1
//2
//Sunday
//{"first":"Albert"}
//300
for (let a of s.values()){
  console.log(a);
}
//1
//2
//Sunday
//{"first":"Albert"}
//300
```

The `keys()` and `values()` iterators both return a list of the unique values in the Set. The `entries()` iterator yields a list of entry arrays, where both items of the array are the unique Set values. The default iterator for a Set is its `values()` iterator.

Symbols

ES6 introduces a new data type called Symbol. A Symbol is guaranteed to be unique and immutable. Symbols are usually used as an identifier for object properties. They can be considered as uniquely generated IDs. You can create Symbols with the `Symbol()` factory method—remember that this is not a constructor and hence you should not use a `new` operator:

```
let s = Symbol();
console.log(typeof s); //symbol
```

Unlike strings, Symbols are guaranteed to be unique and hence help in preventing name clashes. With Symbols, we have an extensibility mechanism that works for everyone. ES6 comes with a number of predefined built-in Symbols that expose various meta behaviors on JavaScript object values.

Iterators

Iterators have been around in other programming languages for quite some time. They give convenience methods to work with collections of data. ES6 introduces iterators for the same use case. ES6 iterators are objects with a specific interface. Iterators have a `next()` method that returns an object. The returning object has two properties—`value` (the next value) and `done` (indicates whether the last result has been reached). ES6 also defines an `Iterable` interface, which describes objects that must be able to produce iterators. Let's look at an array, which is an iterable, and the iterator that it can produce to consume its values:

```
var a = [1,2];
var i = a[Symbol.iterator]();
console.log(i.next());      // { value: 1, done: false }
console.log(i.next());      // { value: 2, done: false }
console.log(i.next());      // { value: undefined, done: true }
```

As you can see, we are accessing the array's iterator via `Symbol.iterator()` and calling the `next()` method on it to get each successive element. Both `value` and `done` are returned by the `next()` method call. When you call `next()` past the last element in the array, you get an undefined value and `done: true`, indicating that you have iterated over the entire array.

For..of loops

ES6 adds a new iteration mechanism in form of the `for..of` loop, which loops over the set of values produced by an iterator.

The value that we iterate over with `for..of` is an iterable.

Let's compare `for..of` to `for..in`:

```
var list = ['Sunday','Monday','Tuesday'];
for (let i in list){
  console.log(i);  //0 1 2
}
for (let i of list){
  console.log(i);  //Sunday Monday Tuesday
}
```

As you can see, using the `for..in` loop, you can iterate over indexes of the `list` array, while the `for..of` loop lets you iterate over the values stored in the `list` array.

Arrow functions

One of the most interesting new parts of ECMAScript 6 is arrow functions. Arrow functions are, as the name suggests, functions defined with a new syntax that uses an *arrow* (`=>`) as part of the syntax. Let's first see how arrow functions look:

```
//Traditional Function
function multiply(a,b) {
  return a*b;
}
//Arrow
var multiply = (a,b) => a*b;
console.log(multiply(1,2)); //2
```

The arrow function definition consists of a parameter list (of zero or more parameters and surrounding `( .. )` if there's not exactly one parameter), followed by the `=>` marker, which is followed by a function body.

The body of the function can be enclosed by { .. } if there's more than one expression in the body. If there's only one expression, and you omit the surrounding { .. }, there's an implied return in front of the expression. There are several variations of how you can write arrow functions. The following are the most commonly used:

```
// single argument, single statement
//arg => expression;
var f1 = x => console.log("Just X");
f1(); //Just X

// multiple arguments, single statement
//(arg1 [, arg2]) => expression;
var f2 = (x,y) => x*y;
console.log(f2(2,2)); //4

// single argument, multiple statements
// arg => {
//     statements;
// }
var f3 = x => {
  if(x>5){
    console.log(x);
  }
  else {
    console.log(x+5);
  }
}
f3(6); //6

// multiple arguments, multiple statements
// ([arg] [, arg]) => {
//    statements
// }
var f4 = (x,y) => {
  if(x!=0 && y!=0){
    return x*y;
  }
}
console.log(f4(2,2));//4
```

```
// with no arguments, single statement
//() => expression;
var f5 = () => 2*2;
console.log(f5()); //4

//IIFE
console.log(( x => x * 3 )( 3 )); // 9
```

It is important to remember that all the characteristics of a normal function parameter are available to arrow functions, including default values, destructuring, and rest parameters.

Arrow functions offer a convenient and short syntax, which gives your code a very *functional programming* flavor. Arrow functions are popular because they offer an attractive promise of writing concise functions by dropping function, return, and { .. } from the code. However, arrow functions are designed to fundamentally solve a particular and common pain point with this-aware coding. In normal ES5 functions, every new function defined its own value of this (a new object in case of a constructor, undefined in strict mode function calls, context object if the function is called as an *object method*, and so on). JavaScript functions always have their own this and this prevents you from accessing the this of, for example, a surrounding method from inside a callback. To understand this problem, consider the following example:

```
function CustomStr(str){
  this.str = str;
}
CustomStr.prototype.add = function(s){    // --> 1
  'use strict';
  return s.map(function (a){               // --> 2
    return this.str + a;                   // --> 3
  });
};

var customStr = new CustomStr("Hello");
console.log(customStr.add(["World"]));
//Cannot read property 'str' of undefined
```

On the line marked with 3, we are trying to get this.str, but the anonymous function also has its own this, which shadows this from the method from line 1. To fix this in ES5, we can assign this to a variable and use the variable instead:

```
function CustomStr(str){
  this.str = str;
}
```

```
CustomStr.prototype.add = function(s){
  'use strict';
  var that = this;                        // --> 1
  return s.map(function (a){              // --> 2
    return that.str + a;                  // --> 3
  });
};


var customStr = new CustomStr("Hello");
console.log(customStr.add(["World"]));
//["HelloWorld]
```

On the line marked with 1, we are assigning this to a variable, that, and in the anonymous function we are using the that variable, which will have a reference to this from the correct context.

ES6 arrow functions have lexical this, meaning that the arrow functions capture the this value of the enclosing context. We can convert the preceding function to an equivalent arrow function as follows:

```
function CustomStr(str){
  this.str = str;
}
CustomStr.prototype.add = function(s){
  return s.map((a)=> {
    return this.str + a;
  });
};
var customStr = new CustomStr("Hello");
console.log(customStr.add(["World"]));
//["HelloWorld]
```

Summary

In this chapter, we discussed a few important features being added to the language in ES6. It's an exciting collection of new language features and paradigms and, using polyfills and transpilers, you can start with them right away. JavaScript is an ever growing language and it is important to understand what the future holds. ES6 features make JavaScript an even more interesting and mature language. In the next chapter, we will dive deep into manipulating the browser's **Document Object Model (DOM)** and events using JavaScript with jQuery.

8

DOM Manipulation
and Events

The most important reason for JavaScript's existence is the web. JavaScript is the language for the web and the browser is the raison d'être for JavaScript. JavaScript gives dynamism to otherwise static web pages. In this chapter, we will dive deep into this relationship between the browser and language. We will understand the way in which JavaScript interacts with the components of the web page. We will look at the **Document Object Model (DOM)** and JavaScript event model.

DOM

In this chapter, we will look at various aspects of JavaScript with regard to the browser and HTML. HTML, as I am sure you are aware, is the markup language used to define web pages. Various forms of markups exist for different uses. The popular marks are **Extensible Markup Language (XML)** and **Standard Generalized Markup Language (SGML)**. Apart from these generic markup languages, there are very specific markup languages for specific purposes such as text processing and image meta information. **HyperText Markup Language (HTML)** is the standard markup language that defines the presentation semantics of a web page. A web page is essentially a document. The DOM provides you with a representation of this document. The DOM also provides you with a means of storing and manipulating this document. The DOM is the programming interface of HTML and allows structural manipulation using scripting languages such as JavaScript. The DOM provides a structural representation of the document. The structure consists of nodes and objects. Nodes have properties and methods on which you can operate in order to manipulate the nodes themselves. The DOM is just a representation and not a programming construct. DOM acts as a model for DOM processing languages such as JavaScript.

Accessing DOM elements

Most of the time, you will be interested in accessing DOM elements to inspect their values or processing these values for some business logic. We will take a detailed look at this particular use case. Let's create a sample HTML file with the following content:

```
<html>
<head>
  <title>DOM</title>
</head>
<body>
  <p>Hello World!</p>
</body>
</html>
```

You can save this file as `sample_dom.html`; when you open this in the Google Chrome browser, you will see the web page displayed with the **Hello World** text displayed. Now, open Google Chrome Developer Tools by navigating to options | **More Tools** | **Developer Tools** (this route may differ on your operating system and browser version). In the **Developer Tools** window, you will see the DOM structure:

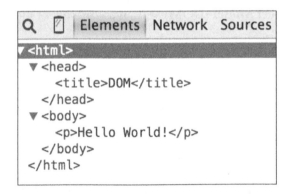

Next, we will insert some JavaScript into this HTML page. We will invoke the JavaScript function when the web page is loaded. To do this, we will call a function on `window.onload`. You can place your script in the `<script>` tag located under the `<head>` tag. Your page should look as follows:

```
<html>
  <head>
    <title>DOM</title>
    <script>
```

```
   // run this function when the document is loaded
   window.onload = function() {
     var doc = document.documentElement;
     var body = doc.body;
     var _head = doc.firstChild;
     var _body = doc.lastChild;
     var _head_ = doc.childNodes[0];
     var title = _head.firstChild;
     alert(_head.parentNode === doc); //true
   }
 </script>
</head>
<body>
 <p>Hello World!</p>
</body>
</html>
```

The anonymous function is executed when the browser loads the page. In the function, we are getting the nodes of the DOM programmatically. The entire HTML document can be accessed using the `document.documentElement` function. We store the document in a variable. Once the document is accessed, we can traverse the nodes using several helper properties of the document. We are accessing the `<body>` element using `doc.body`. You can traverse through the children of an element using the `childNodes` array. The first and last children of a node can be accessed using additional properties—`firstChild` and `lastChild`.

> It is not recommended to use render-blocking JavaScript in the `<head>` tag. This slows down the page render dramatically. Modern browsers support the `async` and `defer` attributes to indicate to the browsers that the rendering can go on while the script is being downloaded. You can use these tags in the `<head>` tag without worrying about performance degradation. You can get more information at `http://stackoverflow.com/questions/436411/where-is-the-best-place-to-put-script-tags-in-html-markup`.

Accessing specific nodes

The core DOM defines the `getElementsByTagName()` method to return `NodeList` of all the element objects whose `tagName` property is equal to a specific value. The following line of code returns a list of all the `<p/>` elements in a document:

```
var paragraphs = document.getElementsByTagName('p');
```

The HTML DOM defines `getElementsByName()` to retrieve all the elements that have their name attribute set to a specific value. Consider the following snippet:

```html
<html>
  <head>
    <title>DOM</title>
    <script>
      showFeelings = function() {
        var feelings = document.getElementsByName("feeling");
        alert(feelings[0].getAttribute("value"));
        alert(feelings[1].getAttribute("value"));
      }
    </script>
  </head>
  <body>
    <p>Hello World!</p>
    <form method="post" action="/post">
      <fieldset>
        <p>How are you feeling today?</p>
        <input type="radio" name="feeling" value="Happy" />
          Happy<br />
        <input type="radio" name="feeling" value="Sad" />Sad<br />
      </fieldset>
      <input type="button" value="Submit"
        onClick="showFeelings()"/>
    </form>
  </body>
</html>
```

In this example, we are creating a group of radio buttons with the `name` attribute defined as `feeling`. In the `showFeelings` function, we get all the elements with the `name` attribute set to `feeling` and we iterate through all these elements.

The other method defined by the HTML DOM is `getElementById()`. This is a very useful method in accessing a specific element. This method does the lookup based on the `id` associated with an element. The `id` attribute is unique for every element and, hence, this kind of lookup is very fast and should be preferred over `getElementsByName()`. -However, you should be aware that the browser does not guarantee the uniqueness of the `id` attribute. In the following example, we are accessing a specific element using the ID. Element IDs are unique as opposed to tags or name attributes:

```html
<html>
  <head>
```

```
    <title>DOM</title>
    <script>
      window.onload= function() {
        var greeting = document.getElementById("greeting");
        alert(greeting.innerHTML); //shows "Hello World" alert
      }
    </script>
  </head>
  <body>
    <p id="greeting">Hello World!</p>
    <p id="identify">Earthlings</p>
  </body>
</html>
```

What we discussed so far was the basics of DOM traversal in JavaScript. When the DOM gets complex and you want sophisticated operations on the DOM, these traversal and access functions seem limiting. With this basic knowledge with us, it's time to get introduced to a fantastic library for DOM traversal (among other things) called jQuery.

jQuery is a lightweight library designed to make common browser operations easier. Common operations such as DOM traversal and manipulation, event handling, animation, and Ajax can be tedious if done using pure JavaScript. jQuery provides you with easy-to-use and shorter helper mechanisms to help you develop these common operations very easily and quickly. jQuery is a feature-rich library, but as far as this chapter goes, we will focus primarily on DOM manipulation and events.

You can add jQuery to your HTML by adding the script directly from a **content delivery network (CDN)** or manually downloading the file and adding it to the script tag. The following example shows you how to download jQuery from Google's CDN:

```
<html>
  <head>
    <script src="https://ajax.googleapis.com/ajax/libs/
      jquery/2.1.4/jquery.min.js"></script>
  </head>
  <body>
  </body>
</html>
```

The advantage of a CDN download is that Google's CDN automatically finds the nearest download server for you and keeps an updated stable copy of the jQuery library. If you wish to download and manually host jQuery along with your website, you can add the script as follows:

```
<script src="./lib/jquery.js"></script>
```

In this example, the jQuery library is manually downloaded in the `lib` directory. With the jQuery setup in the HTML page, let's explore the methods of manipulating the DOM elements. Consider the following example:

```
<html>
  <head>
    <script src="https://ajax.googleapis.com/ajax/libs/
      jquery/2.1.4/jquery.min.js"></script>
    <script>
    $(document).ready(function() {
        $('#greeting').html('Hello World Martian');
    });
  </script>
  </head>
  <body>
    <p id="greeting">Hello World Earthling ! </p>
  </body>
</html>
```

After adding jQuery to the HTML page, we write the custom JavaScript that selects the element with a `greeting` ID and changes its value. The strange-looking code within `$()` is the jQuery in action. If you read the jQuery source code (and you should, it's brilliant) you will see the final line:

```
// Expose jQuery to the global object
window.jQuery = window.$ = jQuery;
```

The `$` is just a function. It is an alias for the function called jQuery. The `$` is a syntactic sugar that makes the code concise. In fact, you can use both `$` and `jQuery` interchangeably. For example, both `$('#greeting').html('Hello World Martian');` and `jQuery('#greeting').html('Hello World Martian');` are the same.

You can't use jQuery before the page is completely loaded. As jQuery will need to know all the nodes of the DOM structure, the entire DOM has to be in-memory. To ensure that the page is completely loaded and in a state where it's ready to be manipulated, we can use the $(document).ready() function. Here, the IIFE is executed only after the entire documented is *ready*:

```
$(document).ready(function() {
    $('#greeting').html('Hello World Martian');
});
```

This snippet shows you how we can associate a function to jQuery's .ready() function. This function will be executed once the document is ready. We are using $(document) to create a jQuery object from our page's document. We are calling the .ready() function on the jQuery object and passing it the function that we want to execute.

This is a very common thing to do when using jQuery—so much so that it has its own shortcut. You can replace the entire ready() call with a short $() call:

```
$(function() {
    $('#greeting').html('Hello World Martian');
});
```

The most important function in jQuery is $(). This function typically accepts a CSS selector as its sole parameter and returns a new jQuery object pointing to the corresponding elements on the page. The three primary selectors are the tag name, ID, and class. They can be used either on their own or in combination with others. The following simple examples illustrate how these three selectors appear in code:

Selector	CSS Selector	jQuery Selector	Output from the selector
Tag	p{}	$('p')	This selects all the p tags from the document.
Id	#div_1	$('#div_1')	This selects single elements that have a div_1 ID. The symbol used to identify the ID is #.
Class	.bold_fonts	$('.bold_fonts')	This selects all the elements in the document that have the CSS class bold_fonts. The symbol used to identify the class match is ".".

jQuery works on CSS selectors.

 As CSS selectors are not in the scope of this book, I would suggest that you go to http://www.w3.org/TR/CSS2/selector.html to get a fair idea of the concept.

We also assume that you are familiar with HTML tags and syntax. The following example covers the fundamental idea of how jQuery selectors work:

```html
<html>
  <head>
    <script src="https://ajax.googleapis.com/ajax/libs/jquery/2.1.4/
jquery.min.js"></script>
    <script>
      $(function() {
        $('h1').html(function(index, oldHTML){
          return oldHTML + "Finally?";
        });
        $('h1').addClass('highlight-blue');
        $('#header > h1 ').css('background-color', 'cyan');
        $('ul li:not(.highlight-blue)').addClass(
          'highlight-green');
        $('tr:nth-child(odd)').addClass('zebra');
      });
    </script>
    <style>
      .highlight-blue {
        color: blue;
      }
      .highlight-green{
        color: green;
      }
      .zebra{
        background-color: #666666;
        color: white;
      }
    </style>
  </head>
  <body>
```

```
<div id=header>
  <h1>Are we there yet ? </h1>
  <span class="highlight">
    <p>Journey to Mars</p>
    <ul>
      <li>First</li>
      <li>Second</li>
      <li class="highlight-blue">Third</li>
    </ul>
  </span>
  <table>
    <tr><th>Id</th><th>First name</th><th>Last Name</th></tr>
    <tr><td>1</td><td>Albert</td><td>Einstein</td></tr>
    <tr><td>2</td><td>Issac</td><td>Newton</td></tr>
    <tr><td>3</td><td>Enrico</td><td>Fermi</td></tr>
    <tr><td>4</td><td>Richard</td><td>Feynman</td></tr>
  </table>
</div>
</body>
</html>
```

In this example, we are selecting several DOM elements in the HTML page using selectors. We have an H1 header with the text, `Are we there yet ?`; when the page loads, our jQuery script accesses all H1 headers and appends the text `Finally?` to them:

```
$('h1').html(function(index, oldHTML){
  return oldHTML + "Finally ?";
});
```

The `$.html()` function sets the HTML for the target element—an H1 header in this case. Additionally, we select all H1 headers and apply a specific CSS style class, `highlight-blue`, to all of them. The `$('h1').addClass('highlight-blue')` statement selects all the H1 headers and uses the `$.addClass(<CSS class>)` method to apply a CSS class to all the elements selected using the selector.

We use the child combinator (`>`) to custom CSS styles using the `$.css()` function. In effect, the selector in the `$()` function is saying, "Find each header (`h1`) that is a child (`>`) of the element with an ID of header (`#header`)." For each such element, we apply a custom CSS. The next usage is interesting. Consider the following line:

```
$('ul li:not(.highlight-blue)').addClass('highlight-green');
```

We are selecting "For all list elements (`li`) that do not have the class `highlight-blue` applied to them, apply CSS class `highlight-green`. The final line —
`$('tr:nth-child(odd)').addClass('zebra')` —can be interpreted as: From all table rows (`tr`), for every odd row, apply CSS style `zebra`. The *n*th-child selector is a custom selector provided by jQuery. The final output looks something similar to the following (Though it shows several jQuery selector types, it is very clear that knowledge of jQuery is not a substitute for bad design taste.):

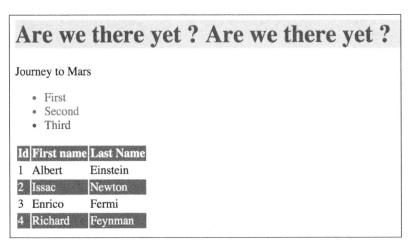

Once you have made a selection, there are two broad categories of methods that you can call on the selected element. These methods are **getters** and **setters**. Getters retrieve a piece of information from the selection, and setters alter the selection in some way.

Getters usually operate only on the first element in a selection while setters operate on all the elements in a selection. Setters use implicit iteration to automatically iterate over all the elements in the selection.

For example, we want to apply a CSS class to all list items on the page. When we call the `addClass` method on the selector, it is automatically applied to all elements of this particular selection. This is implicit iteration in action:

```
$( 'li' ).addClass( highlighted' );
```

However, sometimes you just don't want to go through all the elements via implicit iteration. You may want to selectively modify only a few of the elements. You can explicitly iterate over the elements using the `.each()` method. In the following code, we are processing elements selectively and using the `index` property of the element:

```
$( 'li' ).each(function( index, element ) {
  if(index % 2 == 0)
    $(elem).prepend( '<b>' + STATUS + '</b>' );
});
```

Chaining

Chaining jQuery methods allows you to call a series of methods on a selection without temporarily storing the intermediate values. This is possible because every setter method that we call returns the selection on which it was called. This is a very powerful feature and you will see it being used by many professional libraries. Consider the following example:

```
$( '#button_submit' )
  .click(function() {
    $( this ).addClass( 'submit_clicked' );
  })
  .find( '#notification' )
    .attr( 'title', 'Message Sent' );x
```

In this snippet, we are chaining `click()`, `find()`, and `attr()` methods on a selector. Here, the `click()` method is executed, and once the execution finishes, the `find()` method locates the element with the `notification` ID and changes its `title` attribute to a string.

Traversal and manipulation

We discussed various methods of element selection using jQuery. We will discuss several DOM traversal and manipulation methods using jQuery in this section. These tasks would be rather tedious to achieve using native DOM manipulation. jQuery makes them intuitive and elegant.

Before we delve into these methods, let's familiarize ourselves with a bit of HTML terminology that we will be using from now on. Consider the following HTML:

```
<ul> <-This is the parent of both 'li' and ancestor of everything
  in
  <li> <-The first (li) is a child of the (ul)
    <span>  <-this is the descendent of the 'ul'
      <i>Hello</i>
    </span>
  </li>
  <li>World</li> <-both 'li' are siblings
</ul>
```

Using jQuery traversal methods, we select the first element and traverse through the DOM in relation to this element. As we traverse the DOM, we alter the original selection and we are either replacing the original selection with the new one or we are modifying the original selection.

For example, you can filter an existing selection to include only elements that match a certain criterion. Consider this example:

```
var list = $( 'li' ); //select all list elements
// filter items that has a class 'highlight' associated
var highlighted = list.filter( '.highlight' );
// filter items that doesn't have class 'highlight' associated
var not_highlighted = list.not( '.highlight' );
```

jQuery allows you to add and remove classes to elements. If you want to toggle class values for elements, you can use the `toggleClass()` method:

```
$( '#usename' ).addClass( 'hidden' );
$( '#usename' ).removeClass( 'hidden' );
$( '#usename' ).toggleClass( 'hidden' );
```

Most often, you may want to alter the value of elements. You can use the `val()` method to alter the form of element values. For example, the following line alters the value of all the `text` type inputs in the form:

```
$( 'input[type="text"]' ).val( 'Enter usename:' );
```

To modify element attributes, you can use the `attr()` method as follows:

```
$('a').attr( 'title', 'Click' );
```

jQuery has an incredible depth of functionality when it comes to DOM manipulation — the scope of this book restricts a detailed discussion of all the possibilities.

Working with browser events

When are you developing for browsers, you will have to deal with user interactions and events associated to them, for example, text typed in the textbox, scrolling of the page, mouse button press, and others. When the user does something on the page, an event takes place. Some events are not triggered by user interaction, for example, load event does not require a user input.

When you are dealing with mouse or keyboard events in the browser, you can't predict when and in which order these events will occur. You will have to constantly look for a key press or mouse move to happen. It's like running an endless background loop listening to some key or mouse event to happen. In traditional programming, this was known as polling. There were many variations of these where the waiting thread used to be optimized using queues; however, polling is still not a great idea in general.

Browsers provide a much better alternative to polling. Browsers provide you with programmatic means to react when an event occurs. These hooks are generally called listeners. You can register a listener that reacts to a particular event and executes an associated callback function when the event is triggered. Consider this example:

```
<script>
  addEventListener("click", function() {
    ...
  });
</script>
```

The addEventListener function registers its second argument as a callback function. This callback is executed when the event specified in the first argument is triggered.

What we saw just now was a generic listener for the click event. Similarly, every DOM element has its own addEventListener method, which allows you to listen specifically on this element:

```
<button>Submit</button>
<p>No handler here.</p>
<script>
  var button = document.getElementById("#Bigbutton");
  button.addEventListener("click", function() {
    console.log("Button clicked.");
  });
</script>
```

In this example, we are using the reference to a specific element—a button with a `Bigbutton` ID—by calling `getElementById()`. On the reference of the button element, we are calling `addEventListener()` to assign a handler function for the click event. This is perfectly legitimate code that works fine in modern browsers such as Mozilla Firefox or Google Chrome. On Internet Explorer prior to IE9, however, this is not a valid code. This is because Microsoft implements its own custom `attachEvent()` method as opposed to the W3C standard `addEventListener()` prior to Internet Explorer 9. This is very unfortunate because you will have to write very bad hacks to handle browser-specific quirks.

Propagation

At this point, we should ask an important question—if an element and one of its ancestors have a handler on the same event, which handler will be fired first? Consider the following figure:

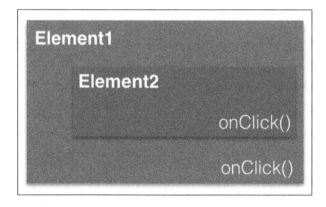

For example, we have **Element2** as a child of **Element1** and both have the `onClick` handler. When a user clicks on Element2, `onClick` on both Element2 and Element1 is triggered but the question is which one is triggered first. What should the event order be? Well, the answer, unfortunately, is that it depends entirely on the browser. When browsers first arrived, two opinions emerged, naturally, from Netscape and Microsoft.

Netscape decided that the first event triggered should be Element1's `onClick`. This event ordering is known as event capturing.

Microsoft decided that the first event triggered should be Element2's `onClick`. This event ordering is known as event bubbling.

These are two completely opposite views and implementations of how browsers handled events. To end this madness, **World Wide Web Consortium (W3C)** decided a wise middle path. In this model, an event is first captured until it reaches the target element and then bubbles up again. In this standard behavior, you can choose in which phase you want to register your event handler—either in the capturing or bubbling phase. If the last argument is true in `addEventListener()`, the event handler is set for the capturing phase, if it is false, the event handler is set for the bubbling phase.

There are times when you don't want the event to be raised by the parents if it was already raised by the child. You can call the `stopPropagation()` method on the event object to prevent handlers further up from receiving the event. Several events have a default action associated with them. For example, if you click on a URL link, you will be taken to the link's target. The JavaScript event handlers are called before the default behavior is performed. You can call the `preventDefault()` method on the event object to stop the default behavior from being triggered.

These are event basics when you are using plain JavaScript on a browser. There is a problem here. Browsers are notorious when it comes to defining event-handling behavior. We will look at jQuery's event handling. To make things easier to manage, jQuery always registers event handlers for the bubbling phase of the model. This means that the most specific elements will get the first opportunity to respond to any event.

jQuery event handling and propagation

jQuery event handling takes care of many of these browser quirks. You can focus on writing code that runs on most supported browsers. jQuery's support for browser events is simple and intuitive. For example, this code listens for a user to click on any button element on the page:

```
$('button').click(function(event) {
  console.log('Mouse button clicked');
});
```

Just like the `click()` method, there are several other helper methods to cover almost all kinds of browser event. The following helpers exist:

* `blur`
* `change`
* `click`
* `dblclick`

- error

- focus

- keydown

- keypress

- keyup

- load

- mousedown

- mousemove

- mouseout

- mouseover

- mouseup

- resize

- scroll

- select

- submit

- unload

Alternatively, you can use the `.on()` method. There are a few advantages of using the `on()` method as it gives you a lot more flexibility. The `on()` method allows you to bind a handler to multiple events. Using the `on()` method, you can work on custom events as well.

Event name is passed as the first parameter to the `on()` method just like the other methods that we saw:

```
$('button').on( 'click', function( event ) {
  console.log(' Mouse button clicked');
});
```

Once you've registered an event handler to an element, you can trigger this event as follows:

```
$('button').trigger( 'click' );
```

This event can also be triggered as follows:

```
$('button').click();
```

You can unbind an event using jQuery's `.off()` method. This will remove any event handlers that were bound to the specified event:

```
$('button').off( 'click' );
```

You can add more than one handler to an element:

```
$("#element")
.on("click", firstHandler)
.on("click", secondHandler);
```

When the event is fired, both the handlers will be invoked. If you want to remove only the first handler, you can use the `off()` method with the second parameter indicating the handler that you want to remove:

```
$("#element).off("click",firstHandler);
```

This is possible if you have the reference to the handler. If you are using anonymous functions as handlers, you can't get reference to them. In this case, you can use namespaced events. Consider the following example:

```
$("#element").on("click.firstclick",function() {
   console.log("first click");
});
```

Now that you have a namespaced event handler registered with the element, you can remove it as follows:

```
$("#element).off("click.firstclick");
```

A major advantage of using `.on()` is that you can bind to multiple events at once. The `.on()` method allows you to pass multiple events in a space-separated string. Consider the following example:

```
$('#inputBoxUserName').on('focus blur', function() {
   console.log( Handling Focus or blur event' );
});
```

You can add multiple event handlers for multiple events as follows:

```
$( "#heading" ).on({
  mouseenter: function() {
    console.log( "mouse entered on heading" );
  },
  mouseleave: function() {
    console.log( "mouse left heading" );
  },
  click: function() {
    console.log( "clicked on heading" );
  }
});
```

As of jQuery 1.7, all events are bound via the `on()` method, even if you call helper methods such as `click()`. Internally, jQuery maps these calls to the `on()` method. Due to this, it's generally recommended to use the `on()` method for consistency and faster execution.

Event delegation

Event delegation allows us to attach a single event listener to a parent element. This event will fire for all the descendants matching a selector even if these descendants will be created in the future (after the listener was bound to the element).

We discussed *event bubbling* earlier. Event delegation in jQuery works primarily due to event bubbling. Whenever an event occurs on a page, the event bubbles up from the element that it originated from, up to its parent, then up to the parent's parent, and so on, until it reaches the root element (`window`). Consider the following example:

```
<html>
  <body>
    <div id="container">
      <ul id="list">
        <li><a href="http://google.com">Google</a></li>
        <li><a href="http://myntra.com">Myntra</a></li>
        <li><a href="http://bing.com">Bing</a></li>
      </ul>
    </div>
  </body>
</html>
```

Now let's say that we want to perform some common action on any of the URL clicks. We can add an event handler to all the a elements in the list as follows:

```
$( "#list a" ).on( "click", function( event ) {
  console.log( $( this ).text() );
});
```

This works perfectly fine, but this code has a minor bug. What will happen if there is an additional URL added to the list as a result of some dynamic action? Let's say that we have an **Add** button that adds new URLs to this list. So, if the new list item is added with a new URL, the earlier event handler will not be attached to it. For example, if the following link is added to the list dynamically, clicking on it will not trigger the handler that we just added:

```
<li><a href="http://yahoo.com">Yahoo</a></li>
```

This is because such events are registered only when the on() method is called. In this case, as this new element did not exist when .on() was called, it does not get the event handler. With our understanding of event bubbling, we can visualize how the event will travel up the DOM tree. When any of the URLs are clicked on, the travel will be as follows:

```
a(click)->li->ul#list->div#container->body->html->root
```

We can create a delegated event as follows:

```
$( "#list" ).on( "click", "a", function( event ) {
  console.log( $( this ).text() );
});
```

We moved a from the original selector to the second parameter in the on() method. This second parameter of the on() method tells the handler to listen to this specific event and check whether the triggering element was the second parameter (the a in our case). As the second parameter matches, the handler function is executed. With this delegate event, we are attaching a single handler to the entire ul#list. This handler will listen to the click event triggered by any descendent of the ul element.

The event object

So far, we attached anonymous functions as event handlers. To make our event handlers more generic and useful, we can create named functions and assign them to the events. Consider the following lines:

```
function handlesClicks(event){
  //Handle click event
}
$("#bigButton").on('click', handlesClicks);
```

Here, we are passing a named function instead of an anonymous function to the `on()` method. Let's shift our focus now to the `event` parameter that we pass to the function. jQuery passes an event object with all the event callbacks. An event object contains very useful information about the event being triggered. In cases where we don't want the default behavior of the element to kick in, we can use the `preventDefault()` method of the event object. For example, we want to fire an AJAX request instead of a complete form submission or we want to prevent the default location to be opened when a URL anchor is clicked on. In these cases, you may also want to prevent the event from bubbling up the DOM. You can stop the event propagation by calling the `stopPropagation()` method of the event object. Consider this example:

```
$( "#loginform" ).on( "submit", function( event ) {
  // Prevent the form's default submission.
  event.preventDefault();
  // Prevent event from bubbling up DOM tree, also stops any
    delegation
  event.stopPropagation();
});
```

Apart from the event object, you also get a reference to the DOM object on which the event was fired. This element can be referred by `$(this)`. Consider the following example:

```
$( "a" ).click(function( event ) {
  var anchor = $( this );
  if ( anchor.attr( "href" ).match( "google" ) ) {
    event.preventDefault();
  }
});
```

Summary

This chapter was all about understanding JavaScript in its most important role — that of browser language. JavaScript plays the role of introducing dynamism on the web by facilitating DOM manipulation and event management on the browser. We discussed both of these concepts with and without jQuery. As the demands of the modern web are increasing, using libraries such as jQuery is essential. These libraries significantly improve the code quality and efficiency and, at the same time, give you the freedom to focus on important things.

We will focus on another incarnation of JavaScript — mainly on the server side. Node.js has become a popular JavaScript framework to write scalable server-side applications. We will take a detailed look at how we can best utilize Node.js for server applications.

9
Server-Side JavaScript

We have been focusing so far on the versatility of JavaScript as the language of the browser. It speaks volumes about the brilliance of the language given that JavaScript has gained significant popularity as a language to program scalable server systems. In this chapter, we will look at Node.js. Node.js is one of the most popular JavaScript frameworks used for server-side programming. Node.js is also one of the most watched project on GitHub and has superb community support.

Node uses V8, the virtual machine that powers Google Chrome, for server-side programming. V8 gives a huge performance benefit to Node because it directly compiles the JavaScript into native machine code over executing bytecode or using an interpreter as a middleware.

The versatility of V8 and JavaScript is a wonderful combination—the performance, reach, and overall popularity of JavaScript made Node an overnight success. In this chapter, we will cover the following topics:

- An asynchronous evented-model in a browser and Node.js
- Callbacks
- Timers
- EventEmitters
- Modules and npm

An asynchronous evented-model in a browser

Before we try to understand Node, let's try to understand JavaScript in a browser.

Node relies on event-driven and asynchronous platforms for server-side JavaScript. This is very similar to how browsers handle JavaScript. Both the browser and Node are event-driven and non-blocking when they use I/O.

To dive deeper into the event-driven and asynchronous nature of Node.js, let's first do a comparison of the various kinds of operations and costs associated with them:

L1 cache read	0.5 nanoseconds
L2 cache read	7 nanoseconds
RAM	100 nanoseconds
Read 4 KB randomly from SSD	150,000 ns
Read 1 MB sequentially from SSD	1,000,000 ns
Read 1 MB sequentially from disk	20,000,000 ns

These numbers are from `https://gist.github.com/jboner/2841832` and show how costly **Input/Output (I/O)** can get. The longest operations taken by a computer program are the I/O operations and these operations slow down the overall program execution if the program keeps waiting on these I/O operations to finish. Let's see an example of such an operation:

```
console.log("1");
var log = fileSystemReader.read("./verybigfile.txt");
console.log("2");
```

When you call `fileSystemReader.read()`, you are reading a file from the filesystem. As we just saw, I/O is the bottleneck here and can take quite a while before the read operation is completed. Depending on the kind of hardware, filesystem, OS, and so on, this operation will block the overall program execution quite a bit. The preceding code does some I/O that will be a blocking operation — the process will be blocked till I/O finishes and the data comes back. This is the traditional I/O model and most of us are familiar with this. However, this is costly and can cause terribly latency. Every process has associated memory and state — both these will be blocked till I/O is complete.

If a program blocks I/O, the Node server will refuse new requests. There are several ways of solving this problem. The most popular traditional approach is to use several threads to process requests—this technique is known as multithreading. If are you familiar with languages such as Java, chances are that you have written multithreaded code. Several languages support threads in various forms—a thread essentially holds its own memory and state. Writing multithreaded applications on a large scale is tough. When multiple threads are accessing a common shared memory or values, maintaining the correct state across these threads is a very difficult task. Threads are also costly when it comes to memory and CPU utilization. Threads that are used on synchronized resources may eventually get blocked.

The browser handles this differently. I/O in the browser happens outside the main execution thread and an event is emitted when I/O finishes. This event is handled by the callback function associated with that event. This type of I/O is non-blocking and asynchronous. As I/O is not blocking the main execution thread, the browser can continue to process other events as they come without waiting on any I/O. This is a powerful idea. Asynchronous I/O allows browsers to respond to several events and allows a high level of interactivity.

Node uses a similar idea for asynchronous processing. Node's event loop runs as a single thread. This means that the application that you write is essentially single-threaded. This does not mean that Node itself is single-threaded. Node uses **libuv** and is multithreaded—fortunately, these details are hidden within Node and you don't need to know them while developing your application.

Every call that involves an I/O call requires you to register a callback. Registering a callback is also asynchronous and returns immediately. As soon as an I/O operation is completed, its callback is pushed on the event loop. It is executed as soon as all the other callbacks that were pushed on the event loop before are executed. All operations are essentially thread-safe, primarily because there is no parallel execution path in the event loop that will require synchronization.

Essentially, there is only one thread running your code and there is no parallel execution; however, everything else except for your code runs in parallel.

Node.js relies on **libev** (http://software.schmorp.de/pkg/libev.html) to provide the event loop, which is supplemented by **libeio** (http://software.schmorp.de/pkg/libeio.html) that uses pooled threads to provide asynchronous I/O. To learn even more, take a look at the libev documentation at http://pod.tst.eu/http://cvs.schmorp.de/libev/ev.pod.

Consider the following example of asynchronous code execution in Node.js:

```
var fs = require('fs');
console.log('1');
fs.readFile('./response.json', function (error, data) {
  if(!error){
    console.log(data);
  });
console.log('2');
```

In this program, we read the `response.json` file from the disk. When the disk I/O is finished, the callback is executed with parameters containing the argument's error, if any error occurred, and data, which is the file data. What you will see in the console is the output of `console.log('1')` and `console.log('2')` one immediately after another:

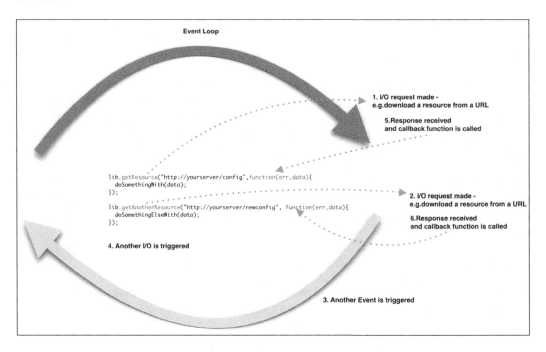

Node.js does not need any additional server component as it creates its own server process. A Node application is essentially a server running on a designated port. In Node, the server and application are the same.

Here is an example of a Node.js server responding with the **Hello Node** string when the `http://localhost:3000/` URL is run from a browser:

```
var http = require('http');
var server = http.createServer();
server.on('request', function (req, res) {
  res.writeHead(200, {'Content-Type': 'text/plain'});
  res.end('Hello Node\n');
});
server.listen(3000);
```

In this example, we are using an `http` module. If you recall our earlier discussions on the JavaScript module, you will realize that this is the CommonJS module implementation. Node has several modules compiled into the binary. The core modules are defined within Node's source. They can be located in the `lib/` folder.

They are loaded first if their identifier is passed to `require()`. For instance, `require('http')` will always return the built-in HTTP module, even if there is a file by this name.

After loading the module to handle HTTP requests, we create a `server` object and use a listener for a `request` event using the `server.on()` function. The callback is called whenever there is a request to this server on port `3000`. The callback receives `request` and `response` parameters. We are also setting the `Content-Type` header and HTTP response code before we send the response back. You can copy the preceding code, save it in a plain text file, and name it `app.js`. You can run the server from the command line using Node.js as follows:

```
$ » node app.js
```

Once the server is started, you can open the `http://localhost:3000` URL in a browser and you will be greeted with unexciting text:

If you want to inspect what's happening internally, you can issue a `curl` command as follows:

```
~ » curl -v http://localhost:3000
* Rebuilt URL to: http://localhost:3000/
*    Trying ::1...
* Connected to localhost (::1) port 3000 (#0)
> GET / HTTP/1.1
> Host: localhost:3000
> User-Agent: curl/7.43.0
> Accept: */*
>
< HTTP/1.1 200 OK
< Content-Type: text/plain
< Date: Thu, 12 Nov 2015 05:31:44 GMT
< Connection: keep-alive
< Transfer-Encoding: chunked
<
Hello Node
* Connection #0 to host localhost left intact
```

Curl shows a nice request (>) and response (<) dialog including the request and response headers.

Callbacks

Callbacks in JavaScript usually take some time getting used to. If you are coming from some other non-asynchronous programming background, you will need to understand carefully how callbacks work; you may feel like you're learning programming for the first time. As everything is asynchronous in Node, you will be using callbacks for everything without trying to carefully structure them. The most important part of the Node.js project is sometimes the code organization and module management.

Callbacks are functions that are executed asynchronously at a later time. Instead of the code reading top to bottom procedurally, asynchronous programs may execute different functions at different times based on the order and speed that earlier functions such as HTTP requests or filesystem reads happen.

Whether a function execution is sequential or asynchronous depends on the context in which it is executed:

```
var i=0;
function add(num){
  console.log(i);
  i=i+num;
}
add(100);
console.log(i);
```

If you run this program using Node, you will see the following output (assuming that your file is named `app.js`):

```
~/Chapter9 » node app.js
0
100
```

This is what we are all used to. This is traditional synchronous code execution where each line is executed in a sequence. The code here defines a function and then on the next line calls this function, without waiting for anything. This is sequential control flow.

Things will be different if we introduced I/O to this sequence. If we try to read something from the file or call a remote endpoint, Node will execute these operations in an asynchronous fashion. For the next example, we are going to use a Node.js module called `request`. We will use this module to make HTTP calls. You can install the module as follows:

```
npm install request
```

We will discuss the use of npm later in this chapter. Consider the following example:

```
var request = require('request');
var status = undefined;
request('http://google.com', function (error, response, body) {
  if (!error && response.statusCode == 200) {
    status_code = response.statusCode;
  }
});
console.log(status);
```

When you execute this code, you will see that the value of the `status` variable is still `undefined`. In this example, we are making an HTTP call—this is an I/O operation. When we do an I/O operation, the execution becomes asynchronous. In the earlier example, we are doing everything within the memory and there was no I/O involved, hence, the execution was synchronous. When we run this program, all of the functions are immediately defined, but they don't all execute immediately. The `request()` function is called and the execution continues to the next line. If there is nothing to execute, Node will either wait for I/O to finish or it will exit. When the `request()` function finishes its work, it will execute the callback function (an anonymous function as the second parameter to the `request()` function). The reason that we got `undefined` in the preceding example is that nowhere in our code exists the logic that tells the `console.log()` statement to wait until the `request()` function has finished fetching the response from the HTTP call.

Callbacks are functions that get executed at some later time. This changes things in the way you organize your code. The idea around reorganizing the code is as follows:

- Wrapping the asynchronous code in a function
- Passing a callback function to the wrapper function

We will organize our previous example with these two ideas in mind. Consider this modified example:

```
var request = require('request');
var status = undefined;
function getSiteStatus(callback){
  request('http://google.com', function (error, response, body) {
    if (!error && response.statusCode == 200) {
      status_code = response.statusCode;
    }
    callback(status_code);
  });
}
function showStatusCode(status){
  console.log(status);
}
getSiteStatus(showStatusCode);
```

When you run this, you will get the following (correct) output:

```
$node app.js
200
```

What we changed was to wrap the asynchronous code in a `getSiteStatus()` function, pass a function named `callback()` as a parameter to this function, and execute this function on the last line of `getSiteStatus()`. The `showStatusCode()` callback function simply wraps around `console.log()` that we called earlier. The difference, however, is in the way the asynchronous execution works. The most important idea to understand while learning how to program with callbacks is that functions are first-class objects that can be stored in variables and passed around with different names. Giving simple and descriptive names to your variables is important in making your code readable by others. Now that the callback function is called once the HTTP call is completed, the value of the `status_code` variable will have a correct value. There are genuine circumstances where you want an asynchronous task executed only after another asynchronous task is completed. Consider this scenario:

```
http.createServer(function (req, res) {
  getURL(url, function (err, res) {
    getURLContent(res.data, function(err,res) {
      . . .
    });
  });
});
```

As you can see, we are nesting one asynchronous function in another. This kind of nesting can result in code that is difficult to read and manage. This style of callback is sometimes known as **callback hell**. To avoid such a scenario, if you have code that has to wait for some other asynchronous code to finish, then you express that dependency by putting your code in functions that get passed around as callbacks. Another important idea is to name your functions instead of relying on anonymous functions as callbacks. We can restructure the preceding example into a more readable one as follows:

```
var urlContentProcessor = function(data){
  . . .
}
var urlResponseProcessor = function(data){
  getURLContent(data,urlContentProcessor);
}
var createServer = function(req,res){
  getURL(url,urlResponseProcessor);
};
http.createServer(createServer);
```

This fragment uses two important concepts. First, we are using named functions and using them as callbacks. Second, we are not nesting these asynchronous functions. If you are accessing closure variables within the inner functions, the preceding would be a bit different implementation. In such cases, using inline anonymous functions is even more preferable.

Callbacks are most frequently used in Node. They are usually preferred to define logic for one-off responses. When you need to respond to repeating events, Node provides another mechanism for this. Before going further, we need to understand the function of timers and events in Node.

Timers

Timers are used to schedule the execution of a particular callback after a specific delay. There are two primary methods to set up such delayed execution: setTimeout and setInterval. The setTimeout() function is used to schedule the execution of a specific callback after a delay, while setInterval is used to schedule the repeated execution of a callback. The setTimeout function is useful to perform tasks that need to be scheduled such as housekeeping. Consider the following example:

```
setTimeout(function() {
  console.log("This is just one time delay");
},1000);
var count=0;
var t = setInterval(function() {
  count++;
  console.log(count);
  if (count> 5){
    clearInteval(t);
  }
}, 2000 );
```

First, we are using setTimeout() to execute a callback (the anonymous function) after a delay of 1,000 ms. This is just a one-time schedule for this callback. We scheduled the repeated execution of the callback using setInterval(). Note that we are assigning the value returned by setInterval() in a variable t — we can use this reference in clearInterval() to clear this schedule.

EventEmitters

We discussed earlier that callbacks are great for the execution of one-off logic. **EventEmitters** are useful in responding to repeating events. EventEmitters fire events and include the ability to handle these events when triggered. Several important Node APIs are built on EventEmitters.

Events raised by EventEmitters are handled through listeners. A listener is a callback function associated with an event—when the event fires, its associated listener is triggered as well. The `event.EventEmitter` is a class that is used to provide a consistent interface to emit (trigger) and bind callbacks to events.

As a common style convention, event names are represented by a camel-cased string; however, any valid string can be used as an event name.

Use `require('events')` to access the `EventEmitter` class:

```
var EventEmitter = require('events');
```

When an EventEmitter instance encounters an error, it emits an `error` event. Error events are treated as a special case in Node.js. If you don't handle these, the program exits with an exception stack.

All EventEmitters emit the `newListener` event when new listeners are added and `removeListener` when a listener is removed.

To understand the usage of EventEmitters, we will build a simplistic telnet server where different clients can log in and enter certain commands. Based on these commands, our server will respond accordingly:

```
var _net = require('net');
var _events = require ('events');
var _emitter = new events.EventEmitter();
_emitter.on('join', function(id,caller){
  console.log(id+" - joined");
});
_emitter.on('quit', function(id,caller){
  console.log(id+" - left");
});
```

```
var _server = _net.createServer(function(caller) {
  var process_id = caller.remoteAddress + ':' + caller.remotePort;
  _emitter.emit('join',id,caller);
  caller.on('end', function() {
    console.log("disconnected");
    _emitter.emit('quit',id,caller);
  });
});
_server.listen(8124);
```

In this code snippet, we are using the `net` module from Node. The idea here is to create a server and let the client connect to it via a standard `telnet` command. When a client connects, the server displays the client address and port, and when the client quits, the server logs this too.

When a client connects, we are emitting a `join` event, and when the client disconnects, we are emitting a `quit` event. We have listeners for both these events and they log appropriate messages on the server.

You start this program and connect to our server using telnet as follows:

```
telnet 127.0.0.1 8124
```

On the server console, you will see the server logging which client joined the server:

```
» node app.js
::ffff:127.0.0.1:51000 - joined
::ffff:127.0.0.1:51001 - joined
```

If any client quits the session, an appropriate message will appear as well.

Modules

When you are writing a lot of code, you soon reach a point where you have to start thinking about how you want to organize the code. Node modules are CommonJS modules that we discussed earlier when we discussed module patterns. Node modules can be published to the **Node Package Manager** (**npm**) repository. The npm repository is an online collection of Node modules.

Creating modules

Node modules can be either single files or directories containing one or more files. It's usually a good idea to create a separate module directory. The file in the module directory that will be evaluated is normally named index.js. A module directory can look as follows:

```
node_project/src/nav
                --- >index.js
```

In your project directory, the nav module directory contains the module code. Conventionally, your module code needs to reside in the index.js file—you can change this to another file if you want. Consider this trivial module called geo.js:

```
exports.area = function (r) {
  return 3.14 * r * r;
};
exports.circumference = function (r) {
  return 3.14 * 3.14 * r;
};
```

You are exporting two functions via exports. You can use the module using the require function. This function takes the name of the module or system path to the module's code. You can use the module that we created as follows:

```
var geo = require('./geo.js');
console.log(geo.area(2));
```

As we are exporting only two functions to the outside world, everything else remains private. If you recollect, we discussed the module pattern in detail—Node uses CommonJS modules. There is an alternative syntax to create modules as well. You can use modules.exports to export your modules. Indeed, exports is a helper created for modules.exports. When you use exports, it attaches the exported properties of a module to modules.exports. However, if modules.exports already has some properties attached to it, properties attached by exports are ignored.

The `geo` module created earlier in this section can be rewritten in order to return a single `Geo` constructor function rather than an object containing functions. We can rewrite the `geo` module and its usage as follows:

```
var Geo = function(PI) {
  this.PI = PI;
}
Geo.prototype.area = function (r) {
  return this.PI * r * r;
};
Geo.prototype.circumference = function (r) {
  return this.PI * this.PI * r;
};
module.exports = Geo;
```

Consider a `config.js` module:

```
var db_config = {
  server: "0.0.0.0",
  port: "3306",
  user: "mysql",
  password: "mysql"
};
module.exports = db_config;
```

If you want to access `db_config` from outside this module, you can use `require()` to include the module and refer the object as follows:

```
var config = require('./config.js');
console.log(config.user);
```

There are three ways to organize modules:

- Using a relative path, for example, `config = require('./lib/config.js')`
- Using an absolute path, for example, `config = require('/nodeproject/lib/config.js')`
- Using a module search, for example, `config = require('config')`

The first two are self-explanatory—they allow Node to look for a module in a particular location in the filesystem.

When you use the third option, you are asking Node to locate the module using the standard look method. To locate the module, Node starts at the current directory and appends `./node_modules/` to it. Node then attempts to load the module from this location. If the module is not found, then the search starts from the parent directory until the root of the filesystem is reached.

For example, if `require('config')` is called in `/projects/node/`, the following locations will be searched until a match a found:

- `/projects/node /node_modules/config.js`
- `/projects/node_modules/config.js`
- `/node_modules/config.js`

For modules downloaded from npm, using this method is relatively simple. As we discussed earlier, you can organize your modules in directories as long as you provide a point of entry for Node.

The easiest way to do this is to create the `./node_modules/supermodule/` directory, and insert an `index.js` file in this directory. The `index.js` file will be loaded by default. Alternatively, you can put a `package.json` file in the `mymodulename` folder, specifying the name and main file of the module:

```
{
  "name": "supermodule",
  "main": "./lib/config.js"
}
```

You have to understand that Node caches modules as objects. If you have two (or more) files requiring a specific module, the first `require` will cache the module in memory so that the second `require` will not have to reload the module source code. However, the second `require` can alter the module functionality if it wishes to. This is commonly called **monkey patching** and is used to modify a module behavior without really modifying or versioning the original module.

npm

The npm is the package manager used by Node to distribute modules. The npm can be used to install, update, and manage modules. Package managers are popular in other languages such as Python. The npm automatically resolves and updates dependencies for a package and hence makes your life easy.

Installing packages

There are two ways to install npm packages: locally or globally. If you want to use the module's functionality only for a specific Node project, you can install it locally relative to the project, which is default behavior of `npm install`. Alternatively, there are several modules that you can use as a command-line tool; in this case, you can install them globally:

```
npm install request
```

The `install` directive with `npm` will install a particular module — `request` in this case. To confirm that `npm install` worked correctly, check to see whether a `node_modules` directory exists and verify that it contains a directory for the package(s) that you installed.

As you start adding modules to your project, it becomes difficult to manage the version/dependency of each module. The best way to manage locally installed packages is to create a `package.json` file in your project.

A `package.json` file can help you in the following ways:

- Defining versions of each module that you want to install. There are times when your project depends on a specific version of a module. In this case, your `package.json` helps you download and maintain the correct version dependency.

- Serving as a documentation of all the modules that your project needs.

- Deploying and packaging your application without worrying about managing dependencies every time you deploy the code.

You can create `package.json` by issuing the following command:

```
npm init
```

After answering basic questions about your project, a blank `package.json` is created with content similar to the following:

```
{
  "name": "chapter9",
  "version": "1.0.0",
  "description": "chapter9 sample project",
  "main": "app.js",
  "dependencies": {
    "request": "^2.65.0"
  },
```

```
  "devDependencies": {},
  "scripts": {
    "test": "echo \"Error: no test specified\" && exit 1"
  },
  "keywords": [
    "Chapter9",
    "sample",
    "project"
  ],
  "author": "Ved Antani",
  "license": "MIT"
}
```

You can manually edit this file in a text editor. An important part of this file is the `dependencies` tag. To specify the packages that your project depends on, you need to list the packages you'd like to use in your `package.json` file. There are two types of packages that you can list:

- `dependencies`: These packages are required by your application in production
- `devDependencies`: These packages are needed only for development and testing (for example, using the **Jasmine node package**)

In the preceding example, you can see the following dependency:

```
"dependencies": {
  "request": "^2.65.0"
},
```

This means that the project is dependent on the `request` module.

 The version of the module is dependent on the semantic versioning rules – `https://docs.npmjs.com/getting-started/semantic-versioning`.

Once your `package.json` file is ready, you can simply use the `npm install` command to install all the modules for your projects automatically.

There is a cool trick that I love to use. While installing modules from the command line, we can add the `--save` flag to add that module's dependency to the `package.json` file automatically:

```
npm install async --save
npm WARN package.json chapter9@1.0.0 No repository field.
npm WARN package.json chapter9@1.0.0 No README data
async@1.5.0 node_modules/async
```

In the preceding command, we installed the `async` module with the normal `npm` command with a `--save` flag. There is a corresponding entry automatically created in `package.json`:

```
"dependencies": {
  "async": "^1.5.0",
  "request": "^2.65.0"
},
```

JavaScript performance

Like any other language, writing correct JavaScript code at scale is an involved task. As the language matures, several of the inherent problems are being taken care of. There are several exceptional libraries that aid in writing good quality code. For most serious systems, *good code = correct code + high performance code*. The demands of new-generation software systems are high on performance. In this section, we will discuss a few tools that you can use to analyze your JavaScript code and understand its performance metrics.

We will discuss the following two ideas in this section:

- Profiling: Timing various functions and operations during script-profiling helps in identifying areas where you can optimize your code
- Network performance: Examining the loading of network resources such as images, stylesheets, and scripts

JavaScript profiling

JavaScript profiling is critical to understand performance aspects of various parts of your code. You can observe timings of the functions and operations to understand which operation is taking more time. With this information, you can optimize the performance of time-consuming functions and tune the overall performance of your code. We will be focusing on the profiling options provided by Chrome's Developer Tools. There are comprehensive analysis tools that you can use to understand the performance metrics of your code.

The CPU profile

The CPU profile shows the execution time spent by various parts of your code. We have to inform DevTools to record the CPU profile data. Let's take the profiler for a spin.

You can enable the CPU profiler in DevTools as follows:

1. Open the Chrome DevTools **Profiles** panel.

2. Verify that **Collect JavaScript CPU Profile** is selected:

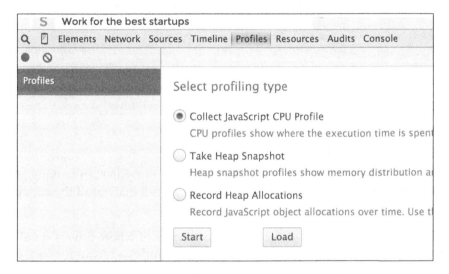

For this chapter, we will be using Google's own benchmark page, `http://octane-benchmark.googlecode.com/svn/latest/index.html`. We will use this because it contains sample functions where we can see various performance bottlenecks and benchmarks. To start recording the CPU profile, open DevTools in Chrome, and in the **Profiles** tab, click on the **Start** button or press *Cmd/Ctrl + E*. Refresh the **V8 Benchmark Suite** page. When the page has completed reloading, a score for the benchmark tests is shown. Return to the **Profiles** panel and stop the recording by clicking on the **Stop** button or pressing *Cmd/Ctrl + E* again.

The recorded CPU profile shows you a detailed view of the functions and the execution time taken by them in the bottom-up fashion, as shown in the following image:

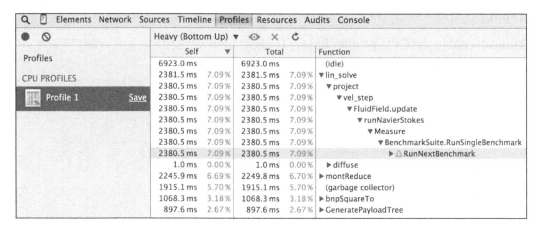

The Timeline view

The Chrome DevTools **Timeline** tool is the first place you can start looking at the overall performance of your code. It lets you record and analyze all the activity in your application as it runs.

The **Timeline** provides you with a complete overview of where time is spent when loading and using your site. A timeline recording includes a record for each event that occurred and is displayed in a **waterfall** graph:

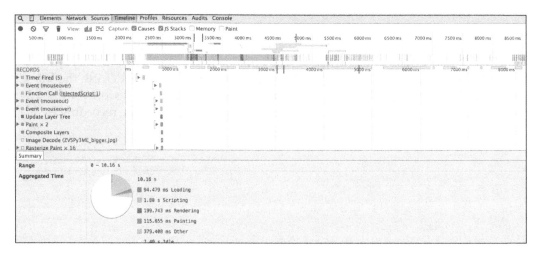

The preceding screen shows you the timeline view when we try to render `https://twitter.com/` in the browser. The timeline view gives you an overall view of which operation took how much time in execution:

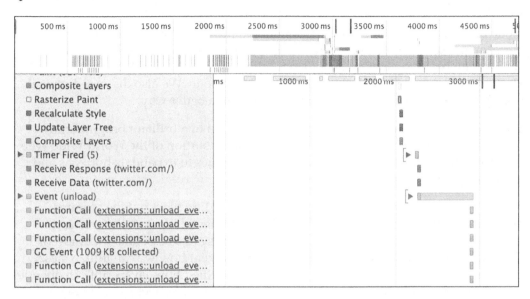

In the preceding screenshot, we can see the progressive execution of various JavaScript functions, network calls, resource downloads, and other operations involved in rendering the Twitter home page. This view gives us a very good idea about which operations may be taking longer. Once we identify such operations, we can optimize them for performance. The **Memory** view is a great tool to understand how the memory is used during the lifetime of your application in the browser. The **Memory** view shows you a graph of the memory used by your application over time and maintains a counter of the number of documents, DOM nodes, and event listeners that are held in the memory. The **Memory** view can help detect memory leaks and give you good enough hints to understand what optimizations are required:

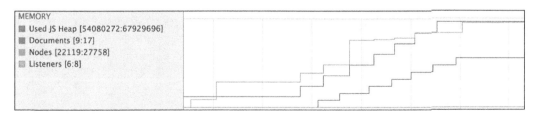

JavaScript performance is a fascinating subject and deserves its own dedicated text. I would urge you to explore Chrome's DevTools and understand how best to use the tools to detect and diagnose performance problems in your code.

Summary

In this chapter, we looked at a different avatar of JavaScript—that of a server-side framework in the form of Node.js.

Node offers an asynchronous evented-model to program scalable and high-performance server applications in JavaScript. We dived deep into some core concepts on Node, such as an event loop, callbacks, modules, and timers. Understanding them is critical to write good Node code. We also discussed several techniques to structure Node code and callbacks in a better way.

With this, we reach the conclusion of our exploration of a brilliant programming language. JavaScript has been instrumental in the evolution of the World Wide Web because of its sheer versatility. The language continues to expand its horizons and improves with each new iteration.

We started our journey with understanding the building blocks of the grammar and syntax of the language. We grasped the fundamental ideas of closures and the functional behavior of JavaScript. These concepts are so essential that most of the JavaScript patterns are based on them. We looked at how we can utilize these patterns to write better code with JavaScript. We studied how JavaScript can operate on a DOM and how to use jQuery to manipulate the DOM effectively. Finally, we looked at the server-side avatar of JavaScript in Node.js.

This book should have enabled you to think differently when you start programming in JavaScript. Not only will you think about common patterns when you code, but also appreciate and use newer language features by ES6.

Index

Symbols

-- operator 17, 18
+ operator 16
++ operator 17, 18
<script> tags
  URL 183
=== strict equality 25, 26
== weak equality 27

A

Agile methodology 146
Amber.js 140
anonymous functions
  about 64
  as parameter to another function 65
  in conditional logic 65, 66
  while creating list 64
  while creating object 64
arguments parameter
  about 60, 61
  this parameter 61
arrow functions 176-179
arrays 86-94
asm.js format 1
asserts 156
asynchronous evented-model
  in browser 202-206
Asynchronous Module Definition
    (AMD) 129
automatic semicolon insertion (ASI)
  about 30, 31
  references 30

B

Babel
  about 164
  URL 164
Backbone.js 139
Backreferences 84, 85
beginning and end 84
Behavior-driven development
    (BDD) 147, 151-153
big.js
  URL 9
block-level scope
  versus function-level scope 52-55
block scopes 56, 57, 165, 166
Boolean operators
  about 18, 21-24
  example 22
  Logical AND 18
  Logical NOT 20
  Logical OR 19
Booleans 13, 14
Bower 90
browser
  asynchronous evented-model 202-206
browser events 193, 194

C

callback hell 209
callbacks 69, 206-210
casting 28
Chai 153
chaining, jQuery methods 191
Chrome DevTools 157
classical inheritance 101

closures 66-70
command line interface (CLI) 41
comments 6
CommonJS modules 129
console.log 156
constants 7
const keyword 7
content delivery network (CDN) 185
controllers 141
CPU profile 219
CSS selectors
  URL 188
curl.js 129

D

date.js
  URL 16
Date object 15, 16
decorator pattern 134-136
design patterns
  about 122
  behavioral 122
  creational 122
  structural 122
Developers Tools (DevTools) 154
Document Object Model (DOM) 179
  about 181
  DOM elements, accessing 182, 183
  specific nodes, accessing 183-190

E

ECMAScript 6 (ES6), syntax changes
  about 56, 165
  arrow functions 176-179
  block scoping 165, 166
  default parameters 167
  destructuring 168, 169
  For..of loops 176
  iterators 175
  Maps 175
  maps and sets 174
  Maps and Sets 172

object literals 170
rest operator 167, 168
Sets 175
spread operator 167, 168
Symbols 175
template literals 171, 172
ECMAScript (ES5) 163
EditorConfig
  URL 32
Emscripten
  URL 1
endsWith() polyfill
  URL 164
equality
  about 25
  strict equality, with === 25, 26
  weak equality, with == 27
Erlang 168
ES6 shim
  URL 164
ES2015 163
eval() method 39
event delegation 198, 199
EventEmitters 211, 212
event object 199
exact match patterns 77
explicit coercion 28
Extensible Markup Language (XML) 181
Extreme Programming 147

F

Facebook React 163
factory pattern 131-133
Firebug 4
For..of loops 176
function context 61
function declarations
  versus function expressions 58-60
function expressions 47
function-level scope
  versus block-level scope 52-55
function literal
  about 46
  function declaration 46-48

functions
  as data 49, 50
function statement 47

G

Gang of Four (GOF) 121
getters 117-120, 190
GitHut
  URL 1
global scope 51
Grave accent
  reference link 12
greedy and lazy quantifiers 85, 86

H

Handlebar.js
  URL 140
Hello World program
  writing 6
hoisting 57
HyperText Markup Language (HTML) 181

I

Immediately Invoked Function Expression
    (IIFE) 55, 165
inheritance 110-116
Input/Output (I/O) 202
instanceof operator 15
instance properties
  versus prototype properties 104-109
IntelliJ WebStorm 154
io.js 1
iterators 175

J

Jasmine
  URL 148, 153
Jasmine node package 217
JavaScript
  history 2
  overview 6
  patterns 121

reference link 2
URL 2
JavaScript debugging
  about 154
  Chrome DevTools 157-161
  console.log and asserts 156
  runtime exceptions 155, 156
  strict, using 155
  syntax errors 154
JavaScript performance
  analyzing 218
  profiling 218
jQuery event handling 195-198
JS Bin
  about 5
  URL 5
  using 5
JSHint 154
  about 41
  running 42
  URL 42
JSLint 154

L

libeio
  URL 203
libev
  URL 203
libuv 203
LiveScript 2
local scope 52
Logical AND Boolean operator 18
Logical NOT Boolean operator 20
Logical OR Boolean operator 19
loops 70
Low-Level Virtual Machine (LLVM)-based
    project 1

M

manipulation methods 191, 192
maps
  about 95, 172
  WeakMap 172, 174

match
  from class of characters 77, 79, 81
mixin pattern 133, 134
Mocha 153 2
models 140
Model-View-Controller (MVC) 139
Model-View-Presenter (MVP)
          pattern 139-142
Model-View-ViewModel
          (MVVM) 139-143
module pattern
  about 124-129
  ES6 modules 131
modules
  about 71, 72, 212
  creating 213, 214
Moment.js
  URL 16
monkey patching 215
Mosaic browser 2
mustache.js
  URL 140
MV* patterns 139

N

namespace pattern 123, 124
NaN (Not a Number) 9
native built-ins
  URL 117
Netscape Navigator 2
Node.js 1, 90, 129, 163, 201
Node Package Manager (npm)
          repository 212
Not Equal To (!==) 26
npm
  about 215
  packages, installing 216-218
Number 8-10

O

object literals 170
object-oriented programming (OOP) 99, 100
objects
  about 99-101
  behavior 101, 102

observer pattern
  about 137-139
  Observer 137
  Subject 137

P

patterns
  about 121
  decorator pattern 134-136
  design patterns 122, 123
  factory pattern 131-133
  mixin pattern 133, 134
  module pattern 124-130
  namespace pattern 123, 124
  observer pattern 137-139
polyfills 164
private variables 69, 70
profiling, JavaScript
  about 218
  CPU profile 219
  Timeline view 220, 221
propagation
  about 194, 195
  jQuery event handling 195-198
prototype
  about 103, 104
  properties, versus instance
          properties 104-109

R

Read-Eval-Print-Loop (REPL)
  about 4
  URL 164
RegEx (regular expressions) 76, 77
repeated occurrences
  about 81-83
  Alternatives - OR 84
RequireJS
  URL 130
revealing module pattern (RMP) 127
router 141

S

Scheme 2

scoping
  about 50
  block scopes 56
  function-level scope versus block-level
    scope 52-55
  global scope 51
  inline function expressions 56
  local scope 52
semantic versioning
  URL 217
sets 95, 96, 173
setters 117-120, 190
shims 164
Silverlight 142
simple patterns 77
Sinon.JS 153
sloppy mode 39
special characters 11
Spies 152
Stack Overflow
  URL 9
Standard Generalized Markup Language
  (SGML) 181
strict equality 25, 26
strict mode
  about 39, 40, 155
  blocked features 41
  enabling 40
  eval() function 41
  using 40
  variables, declaring 40
string 11, 12
style guide
  about 32
  braces 32
  conditional evaluation 36
  empty line 34
  end of line 34
  eval() method 39
  JSHint 41, 42
  line breaks 32
  naming 38
  parentheses 32
  quotes 34
  strict mode 39, 40
  type, casting 35, 36
  type, checking 35

white spaces 32
styling
  considerations 72, 97
subtypes 27

T

tagged template string 172
tags 27
template literals 171, 172
Test-driven development (TDD) 147
TestPyramid
  URL 147
this parameter
  invocation, as constructor 63
  invocation, as function 61
  invocation, as method 61-63
  invocation, call() methods used 63
Timeline view 220, 221
timers 69, 210
Timezone.js
  URL 16
Tool Command Language (TCL) 2
transpilers 164
traversal methods 191, 192
typeof operator 15
types 27-30

U

undefined values 13
Underscore.js
  about 119, 134
  URL 90
unit testing
  about 146
  Behavior-driven development
    (BDD) 147-152
  Test-driven development (TDD) 147

V

V8 201
Value Added Tax (VAT) 9
variables 7
var keyword 7
views 140, 141

W

waterfall graph 220
weak equality 27
WeakMap 172-174
WeakSet 172
Windows Presentation Foundation
        (WPF) 142
World Wide Web Consortium (W3C) 195

Thank you for buying
Mastering JavaScript

About Packt Publishing

Packt, pronounced 'packed', published its first book, *Mastering phpMyAdmin for Effective MySQL Management*, in April 2004, and subsequently continued to specialize in publishing highly focused books on specific technologies and solutions.

Our books and publications share the experiences of your fellow IT professionals in adapting and customizing today's systems, applications, and frameworks. Our solution-based books give you the knowledge and power to customize the software and technologies you're using to get the job done. Packt books are more specific and less general than the IT books you have seen in the past. Our unique business model allows us to bring you more focused information, giving you more of what you need to know, and less of what you don't.

Packt is a modern yet unique publishing company that focuses on producing quality, cutting-edge books for communities of developers, administrators, and newbies alike. For more information, please visit our website at www.packtpub.com.

About Packt Open Source

In 2010, Packt launched two new brands, Packt Open Source and Packt Enterprise, in order to continue its focus on specialization. This book is part of the Packt Open Source brand, home to books published on software built around open source licenses, and offering information to anybody from advanced developers to budding web designers. The Open Source brand also runs Packt's Open Source Royalty Scheme, by which Packt gives a royalty to each open source project about whose software a book is sold.

Writing for Packt

We welcome all inquiries from people who are interested in authoring. Book proposals should be sent to author@packtpub.com. If your book idea is still at an early stage and you would like to discuss it first before writing a formal book proposal, then please contact us; one of our commissioning editors will get in touch with you.

We're not just looking for published authors; if you have strong technical skills but no writing experience, our experienced editors can help you develop a writing career, or simply get some additional reward for your expertise.

HTML5 Boilerplate Web Development

ISBN: 978-1-84951-850-5   Paperback: 174 pages

Master Web Development with a robust set of templates to get your projects done quickly and effectively

1. Master HTML5 Boilerplate as starting templates for future projects.

2. Learn how to optimize your workflow with HTML5 Boilerplate templates and set up servers optimized for performance.

3. Learn to feature-detect and serve appropriate styles and scripts across browser types.

Mastering JavaScript Design Patterns

ISBN: 978-1-78398-798-6   Paperback: 290 pages

Discover how to use JavaScript design patterns to create powerful applications with reliable and maintainable code

1. Learn how to use tried and true software design methodologies to enhance your Javascript code.

2. Discover robust JavaScript implementations of classic as well as advanced design patterns.

3. Packed with easy-to-follow examples that can be used to create reusable code and extensible designs.

Please check **www.PacktPub.com** for information on our titles

open source
community experience distilled

[PACKT]
PUBLISHING

Learning JavaScriptMVC

ISBN: 978-1-78216-020-5   Paperback: 124 pages

Learn to build well-structured JavaScript web applications using JavaScriptMVC

1. Install JavaScriptMVC in three different ways, including installing using Vagrant and Chef.

2. Document your JavaScript codebase and generate searchable API documentation.

3. Test your codebase and application as well as learning how to integrate tests with the continuous integration tool, Jenkins.

Mastering JavaScript High Performance

ISBN: 978-1-78439-729-6   Paperback: 208 pages

Master the art of building, deploying, and optimizing faster web applications with JavaScript

1. Test and optimize JavaScript code efficiently.

2. Build faster and more proficient JavaScript programs for web browsers and hybrid mobile apps.

3. Step-by-step tutorial stuffed with real-world examples.

Please check **www.PacktPub.com** for information on our titles

96755312R00137

Made in the USA
Columbia, SC
01 June 2018